WADSWORTH PHILOSOPHERS SERIES

D0723272

ON

AYER

Robert M. Martin
Dalhousie University, Halifax, Nova Scotia

WADSWORTH

™

THOMSON LEARNING

Australia • Canada • Mexico • Singapore • Spain
United Kingdom • United States

WADSWORTH

THOMSON LEARNING ™

Grateful thanks to Sheldon Wein and Frances Martin,
who read this book in manuscript and made many
helpful suggestions.

Printed in the United States of America
1 2 3 4 5 6 7 04 03 02 01 00

For permission to use material from this text, contact us:
Web: http://www.thomsonrights.com
Fax: 1-800-730-2215
Phone: 1-800-730-2214

For more information, contact:
Wadsworth/Thomson Learning, Inc.
10 Davis Drive
Belmont, CA 94002-3098
USA
http://www.wadsworth.com

ISBN: 0-534-58370-9

Contents

"The trouble with Freddie Ayer is that he is clever all the time."
  —Ludwig Wittgenstein

"Ayer est un con."
  —Jean-Paul Sartre

1

Introduction

Some people think that philosophy is where you go for answers to the Big Questions: What is the meaning of life? Where did everything come from? What is the nature of reality? How should one live? Philosophy is supposed to provide wisdom, maybe comfort in times of trouble, perhaps a "philosophical attitude" of equanimity, calmness, detachment, serenity. But "analytic" philosophy the brand of philosophy that has been dominant in the English-speaking world for most of the twentieth century, is a big disappointment in all these respects. This is not because analytic philosophy tries to provide these things and fails; it is because most analytic philosophers have decided that philosophy cannot legitimately claim to provide any of these things, and should not even try. Analytic philosophers believe that the jobs philosophy can do are entirely different ones, far less sweeping in their pretension, more technical, and, sadly, less attractive to many non-philosophers. These jobs are, roughly speaking, the analysis of concepts and language, the drawing out of their implications and applications, their clarification and disambiguation. To answer questions about the way things really are out there in the real world is seen either as the job of empirical science, or else as nobody's job, because if factual questions cannot be answered by science, then nobody can answer them.

This radical analytic minimizing view had its historical roots in the thought of the British empiricists John Locke (1632-1702), David Hume (1711-1776), and John Stuart Mill (1806-1873). During the first third of the twentieth century, these empiricist ideas were developed by Bertrand Russell and G.E. Moore at Cambridge University in England, by a group of philosophers, scientists, and mathematicians meeting in

Vienna (the "Vienna Circle"), and by Ludwig Wittgenstein, who influenced both the Vienna Circle and the Cambridge philosophers. But then, rather suddenly, these ideas took over English-speaking philosophy in a profound revolution whose effects are still very much with us. The start of this revolution can be precisely dated at 1936, the year of the publication of A. J. Ayer's book *Language, Truth and Logic*.[1] It was this book that brought together, lucidly and forcefully, the central ideas of the empiricist tradition and defined the analytic school. The book became a best-seller, and converted a large proportion of younger philosophers to its views. It was the most influential work of English-language philosophy of the century.

Ayer's book, like many revolutionary tracts, was the enthusiastic work of youth. Within a few years, it began to appear even to the most enthusiastic analytic philosophers and to Ayer himself that some of its positions were inadequate, and should at least be refined, if not rejected. During the rest of his long philosophical career, he continued to work on the same family of philosophical problems, sometimes defending his *LTL* views, sometimes amending them. Enormously prolific, Ayer produced important philosophical writing until his death in 1989. All of his writing after *LTL* shared that book's lucidity and persuasive power, but none of it had the bombshell revolutionary force of his first book.

When we look at his work, we shall obviously pay a good deal of attention to the origins, content, and impact of *LTL*; but we shall not ignore the work he did later, which is important in a much less dramatic way, showing Ayer not so much as the messiah of a new movement, but rather as an important, careful and more cautious philosopher.

Ayer was an unusual person, with an interesting life. We shall start with a bit of biography, then move on to consideration of his philosophy.

---

[1] First Edition (London: Victor Gollancz, 1936). Page references will be to the Revised (Second) edition, from the same publisher, 1946. In what follows, this book will be referred to as *LTL*.

2
Biography

Family and Childhood Influences

Ayer grew up in England, but his parents were both foreign-born. His father Jules moved to London from Switzerland at seventeen. His mother Reine came from a Dutch Jewish background; her father, a successful car manufacturer, took her to London when quite young. Their only child, Alfred Jules Ayer, was born in 1910. He was named after his godfather, the banker Alfred Rothschild, for whom his father was working as private secretary. (Ayer always hated the name Alfred, and invariably encouraged his friends and even his students to call him Freddie.)

When Ayer was about eighteen months old, his father went bankrupt, due to failed currency speculations and perhaps gambling, and Rothschild, who disapproved of financial speculation, fired him. Jules's father-in-law paid his debts and bought him a partnership in a firm of timber merchants; the firm flourished, but Jules disliked his work, and he and the family felt that he was a failure. Even as a young child, Ayer felt a good deal of family pressure to succeed (he reports that his grandfather had hopes that he would become Prime Minister). Despite his demonstration of considerable aptitude at school and his great success later on in his academic career, he continued to feel that he was a disappointment to his family. Like many children driven by family ambitions, he felt that his achievements were never quite good enough.

Ayer refers to himself as an abnormal boy. He was very short, slim, and delicate, incompetent at most sports and clumsy (he never learned to build anything with his Meccano set or to ride a bicycle); bookish and adult-oriented, with very few friends among other children (though he claims not have been lonely); an intellectually precocious child, sensitive, "unusually susceptible to childish terrors,"[1] high-strung, enthusiastic and perceptive, a fast and glib talker, somewhat spoiled, a bit of a showoff, and probably rather a pain in the neck.

A recent biographer, having interviewed many of his family and friends, believes that the Ayer household was a "joyless and unstimulating place to grow up,"[2] and that he had a "bleak and difficult upbringing, one that hurt and in some ways limited him."[3] His parents' marriage was unhappy; his father drank heavily, and his mother had an empty life, with too little to do. In his autobiography Ayer represents his childhood as on the whole a happy one, but perhaps he did not want to complain in print. He hints at having adopted an "affectation of indifference" to unhappiness or rejection,[4] and rarely showed his feelings.

School Days

At age seven, Ayer was sent away to a "barbarous"[5] boy's prep-school, Ascham St Vincent's, where he was "dreadfully unhappy."[6] He speaks of having been bullied, surprisingly "not because I was known to be partly Jewish but because I had confessed to being partly Swiss."[7] Can one trust his report of the first instance on record of English anti-Swissism? The school was not academically strong, and tended to emphasize sports instead. Ayer was not good at most sports, but at about the time he entered Ascham, he developed what was to be a lifelong passionate interest in following professional soccer and cricket.

The sole function of schools like Ascham, according to Ayer, was to achieve admission for its students into the best English public schools; and, in his case it worked. At age twelve, he won a scholarship to Eton. He was initially reluctant to take his place there, believing that it was "a snobbish school in which I should be out of place,"[8] but his

---

[1] A. J. Ayer, *Part of My Life: The Memoirs of a Philosopher* (London: Collins, 1977) 21. This book, the first volume of Ayer's autobiography, will be referred to from now on as *PML*.

[2] *PML* 18.

[3] Ben Rogers, *A. J. Ayer: A Life* (London: Chatto & Windus, 1999) 9.

[4] *PML* 57-8.

[5] Rogers 24.

[6] Rogers 25.

[7] A. J. Ayer, "My Mental Development," Lewis E. Hahn, Ed., *The Philosophy of A. J. Ayer* (La Salle, IL: Open Court, 1992) 5. This article is referred to below as "MMD."

[8] "MMD" 6.

grandfather persuaded him that attendance at Eton "would be a source of future advantages which it would be stupid of me to forgo. On the whole, I think he was right."[9] Clearly Eton put him on the path to the education and the social contacts that, given his substantial talent, would provide him with the assurance of a comfortable future.

He regards his unhappiness at Eaton as his own fault:

> There was much to enjoy at Eton. If I was in the main not happy there, except in my first and final years, it was because I got on badly with the other boys in College. This was very largely my own fault. I was too pleased with my own cleverness and I had a sarcastic tongue.[10]

He was especially annoyingly sarcastic about religion. He did not have a religious background. The maternal side of his family was not ashamed of its Jewish heritage, but was decidedly assimilationist and rationalistically anti-religious. His father was nominally Calvinist, but had only the vaguest of religious belief, if any. Ayer's parents never went to church and gave him no religious training except for teaching him to say prayers at night before going to bed:

> a practice which I continued until about the age of twelve. I had a utilitarian attitude to prayer, and came to doubt its efficacy when it failed to get me into the cricket eleven of my preparatory school.[11]

As a teenager at Eaton, he halfheartedly participated in the required religious practice and study, and for the first time gave some serious thought to religious belief and decided it was "intellectually untenable."[12]

Eaton required that students choose a field to concentrate in. Ayer was inclined toward history, but chose classics instead, believing that this specialization, with less competition than history, would help him win a scholarship to Oxford or Cambridge. His studies went well, apparently without a great deal of effort on his part, and he won a scholarship to Christ Church College, Oxford, and entered there in 1929.

---

[9] "MMD" 6.
[10] *PML* 57.
[11] *PML* 16-17.
[12] "MMD" 9.

Oxford

The early thirties was an exciting time to be an Oxford student. They still enjoyed the traditional privileges of an earlier age, but were no longer bound by Victorian puritanism. Experimentation and hedonism, progressive politics, avant-garde art, and sexual freedom were in the air. Ayer later talked of his years at Oxford as a liberation. His interests in literature and art flourished. He made a wide circle of good friends, and had his first lover, Renée Lees, a very pretty, intelligent, adventurous, and difficult woman.

By the time he entered Oxford in 1929, Ayer had already developed some interest in philosophy, stemming from his love of painting. He had read Clive Bell's book *Art*,[13] in which Bell asserts that 'good' is indefinable, and points to G. E. Moore's *Principia Ethica*[14] for proof of this; Ayer read Moore's book and was convinced. Somewhere around then, he also read Bertrand Russell's *Sceptical Essays*, the opening sentences of which were, he says, to serve him as a motto throughout his philosophical career:

> I wish to propose for the reader's favorable consideration a doctrine which may, I fear, appear wildly paradoxical and subversive. The doctrine in question is this: that it is undesirable to believe a proposition when there is no ground whatever for supposing it true.[15]

Having grown tired of classical study after only one term, he got permission to switch to "Greats" which was primarily ancient history and philosophy.

"The dominant tone of Oxford philosophy at that time," Ayer recalls, "was surly and unadventurous."[16] The Oxford philosophers were mostly backward-looking old fashioned historians. An exception, however, was Gilbert Ryle, who had recently become disillusioned with his earlier specialization in the German phenomenologists, and had turned instead to the work of Russell and C. D. Broad at Cambridge. Ryle introduced Ayer to Ludwig Wittgenstein's *Tractatus Logico-Philosophicus*,[17] which had had almost no attention outside Cambridge. Ayer was captivated, and decided to abandon his plans to use his Greats

---

[13] (London: Chatto & Windus, 1914).

[14] (Cambridge: Cambridge UP, 1903).

[15] (London: Unwin Books, 1935) 1.

[16] *PML* 77.

[17] (London: Routledge & Kegan Paul, 1922).

degree as a foundation for a career in law, and rather to continue on in philosophy.

Before he completed his degree, Christ Church College appointed him to succeed a lecturer who had applied for a professorship elsewhere. But the lecturer did not obtain the position and remained at Oxford, so Ayer was not needed as tutor, and he was given a two term leave of absence. His plan was to spend this leave learning from Wittgenstein in Cambridge, but Ryle had been impressed by the Viennese philosopher Mauritz Schlick at a conference a while back, and thought it would be a good idea for Ayer to go find out what was going on in Vienna. Ayer agreed, because he was planning on getting married and thought that Vienna would be a good place to spend his honeymoon.

The Vienna Circle

Ayer and Renée were married and went off to Vienna. When they arrived, Ayer looked up Schlick, who invited him to attend some meetings of his philosophy discussion group. It included the philosophers Otto Neurath, and Friedrich Waismann, (with occasional visits by W. V. Quine), the mathematicians Karl Menger and Hans Hahn, and the logician Kurt Gödel. Rudolf Carnap, Hans Reichenbach, and Wittgenstein had earlier attended discussions, and had left a strong influence on them. They called themselves the Vienna Circle.

Members of the Circle were by then reaching a good deal of philosophical agreement, and saw themselves increasingly as a revolutionary philosophical movement. Logical Positivism, as their movement came to be known, would discard all the overblown wooly pretentious nonsense that had passed as philosophy for centuries. It stood for reason, clarity, and science, against romanticism, emotionality, religion, and superstition, and for left-wing egalitarian socialistic politics and morality.

Ayer returned to Oxford in the spring of 1933, with enormous— one might even say, religious—enthusiasm for what he had learned. He produced five published papers and some conference talks on the subject in nine months. His new ideas startled and offended the philosophical old guard, condemning large amounts of their work as meaningless, and predicting the death of their outdated philosophical methods. He had a few defenders in the Oxford department, but there was a good deal of displeasure, and he was passed over for a permanent appointment.

Ayer's friend Isaiah Berlin advised him to "get it all written down before [his] enthusiasm had been given time to stale."[18] Ayer thought he should write a book, but, with typical cocky arrogance, wanted assurance of publication before he began work on this large project. A woman he knew got him an interview with the publisher Victor Gollancz. Ayer explained to Gollancz that the book he was planning would be the most important philosophical work in decades, and would contain definitive solutions for every outstanding philosophical problem. Gollancz gave him a contract (possibly just to get Ayer out of his office.) He started writing in December 1933, and nineteen months later, at age 24, he had finished *Language, Truth and Logic.*

Language, Truth and Logic

The ideas in Ayer's book were hardly original; just about everything in there can be traced either to the Vienna Circle or to Russell, Moore, and their Cambridge group.[19] Its positions became subject to widespread and effective criticism immediately after publication. When asked during the mid-1970s what he thought were the defects of the book, Ayer answered, "Well, I suppose the most important defect was that nearly all of it was false."[20] But Ayer's book was the most influential English-language philosophy publication of the century.

One reason for its wide influence was that it had appeared at exactly the right time. The 1930s was a decade for youthful rebellion against bourgeois conventions and old certainties, and the English-speaking philosophy establishment was ripe for a shake-up. Oxford philosophy was uninspiring. At Cambridge, Russell and Moore had said their piece, and were no longer doing much; there was some interesting discussion of Wittgenstein's *Tractatus* at Cambridge, but these new ideas had not spread. Almost nothing was happening at the rest of the British universities. American philosophy was in the thrall of the builders of huge speculative metaphysical edifices: Dewey, Whitehead, Santayana. Ayer's book synthesized what was developing in Cambridge and Vienna, and got the word out to the philosophical world,

---

[18] *PML* 154.

[19] An account of the sources of Ayer's main ideas can be found in "Ayer's Place in the History of Philosophy" by Anthony Quinton, in *A. J. Ayer: Memorial Essays*, A. Phillips Griffiths, ed. (Cambridge: Cambridge UP, 1991) 31-48.

[20] Interviewed by Bryan Magee, "Logical Positivism and its Legacy," in Bryan Magee, *Men of Ideas* (Oxford: Oxford UP, 1982) 107.

which gobbled the book up. It was probably the most widely read British philosophical book in 25 years.[21]

The book is beautifully written, in Ayer's lucid and elegant prose. It is brief—only about 60,000 words—but comprehensive, covering the implications of its basic philosophical principles on all the main areas of philosophical concern. It was an exciting exhilarating revolutionary work, full of fervor and enthusiasm. It raised a storm of opposition, achieved cult status among young intellectuals, and eventually revolutionized philosophical practice in the English-speaking world.

Politics, Friends, and Lovers

Anthony Quinton writes:

> Ayer always thought of himself as Russell's successor. He modeled his thought on that of Russell, both in its content and in its unguarded expression and also, to some extent, his manner of life, both political and amorous.[22]

Ayer reports having had vague leftist sympathies as a youth, but the Spanish Civil War roused him to a more lively political consciousness. Isaiah Berlin recalls that Ayer "was always ready to quarrel about politics. If he thought that someone was pro-Franco he would cross the street to strike them."[23] He read a great deal of political theory, lectured on the subject at Oxford, and intended to write a book on it; but this was abandoned when he found that he had little substantial to say. He began to work with the local branch of the Labour Party in London; he made some street-corner speeches (very uncomfortably), wrote an inflammatory pamphlet, and ran unsuccessfully for Westminister City Council in 1937. Communism was popular among intellectuals in those days, and friends urged Ayer to join the Communist Party, but

> I declined to join on the grounds that I did not believe in dialectical materialism...It did seem to me that if one was to join the Communist Party, one ought at least to believe in its underlying theory... I had more sympathy for the outlook of John Stuart Mill than for that of Lenin.[24]

---

[21] Quinton claims "No British philosophical book since Russell's *[The] Problem[s] of Philosophy* (1912) can have been as widely read" (Quinton 41).

[22] Quinton 31.

[23] Rogers 132.

[24] *PML* 187.

Ayer was no political radical, but his liberal political sympathies were strong and he worked energetically, at times, on political causes.

By the early 1940s, Ayer had developed from a rather solitary child into a gregarious socializer. Fellow students at Oxford were impressed with his literary and artistic sophistication, and he was to become comfortable not only with the intellectual, but also with the cultural and artistic elite, as shown by this impressive (but partial) list of his non-philosopher friends and acquaintances: W. H. Auden, Lauren Bacall, Tallulah Bankhead, Clive Bell, John Betjeman, Jacob Bronowski, Albert Camus, Raymond Chandler, Charlie Chaplin, Randolph Churchill, John Cleese, Jean Cocteau, Lucien Freud, Cyril Connolly, E. E. Cummings, T. S. Eliot, Alberto Giacometti, Graham Greene, Frankie Howerd, Aldous Huxley, Christopher Isherwood, Arthur Koestler, Irving Krystol, Elsa Lanchester, Charles Laughton, C. S. Lewis, Somerset Maugham, Iris Murdoch, Malcolm Muggerage, Lawrence Olivier, George Orwell, Stephen Spender, Gertrude Stein, Philip Toynbee, Hugh Trevor-Roper, Andy Warhol, Evelyn Waugh, Rebecca West, Thornton Wilder, Virginia Woolf.[25]

Quinton speaks of Ayer's "amorous" resemblance to Russell, who shocked conservative moralists when he wrote in 1929 that "where a marriage is fruitful and both parties to it are reasonable and decent, the expectation ought to be that it will be lifelong, but not that it will exclude other sex relations."[26] Ayer's autobiography reveals a certain latitude in his sexual morality, and an offhandedness that some would find distressing; for example:

> My life with Renée had begun to go awry. Some months before, at the end of a winter term, I was sharing a taxi on the way to Oxford station with a girl whom I knew only slightly when it suddenly became clear that we wanted one another. I immediately told the driver to turn back, took the girl to my rooms, and made love to her... After that I engaged in a series of affairs which I concealed from Renée, but could not conceal from her that something was amiss. ... It was distressing to me but also something of a relief to my conscience when Renée,

---

[25] This list was compiled from his two autobiographies. One literary figure who (for a change) apparently did *not* know Ayer was C. P. Snow. An excerpt from a review of *PML* by Snow, printed on its dustjacket, praises "Sir Frederick Ayer's first installment of autobiography." Freddie Ayer was nevertheless Sir *Alfred* Ayer.

[26] *Marriage and Morals* (London: Unwin Paperbacks, 1976) 95.

with her deeper nature, became seriously attracted to a friend of mine, a younger man who was very much in love with her. He told me of it but I treated his confession lightly. In the Christmas holidays the three of us went to Paris together, but finding the strain too great, I soon returned alone. ...For once I felt a little sorry for myself but I soon plunged into a round of parties and was cheerful enough by the time that Renée returned.[27]

The unnamed friend who was in love with Renée was Ayer's colleague Stuart Hampshire. A few months later, Ayer began another affair, and shortly thereafter, he traveled alone to the U.S.; a few months after his return, Renée was pregnant, and it was clear that Hampshire was the father. Ayer and Renée remained together, though apparently both continued having affairs.

After *LTL*

By the end of 1939, Ayer had finished writing his second book *The Foundations of Empirical Knowledge*.[28] In this work Ayer reveals second thoughts about his radical views expressed in *LTL*, qualifying and sometimes rejecting them. He says that he found the reviews of *FEK* on the whole favorable, though he reports that his friend John Wisdom wrote that the book showed "the disastrous effects of qualms upon an iconoclast."[29]

Before the book was released, in 1940, Ayer decided that he should be doing something for the British war effort, and he enlisted in the army. He was placed in officer's training, which he appears to have enjoyed somewhat; his autobiography makes this sound a bit like summer camp. Perhaps he was, as usual, refraining from complaining in print; but England's army training then does appears to have been easy-going and tolerant of Ayer's eccentricity. With a trace of self-mockery, Ayer tells that one day when bad weather forced cancellation of the planned activities, it was suggested that Ayer put on a lecture.

> I thought it best to stick to my own subject, and chose therefore to lecture on Berkeley's Idealism. The view that material objects, including their own bodies and the bullets that might enter them, were nothing but collections of ideas was novel to

---

[27] *PML* 205.

[28] (London: Macmillan, 1940). This will be abbreviated as *FEK*.

[29] Ayer quotes this in *PML* 220, but he does not give its source.

> most of my audience, and even roused one or two of them to
> indignation, but the lecture was generally well received.[30]

His training complete, Ayer began a series of assignments in the army: as a trainer of recruits, then as an interrogator of German prisoners, then as a sort of domestic spy, with the job of sitting around in pubs chatting and overhearing conversations. In 1941, he was sent to New York to work in a highly secretive organization collecting intelligence and plotting international clandestine operations; but all Ayer was to do was to write summaries of others' reports.

The army never knew exactly how to make use of Ayer, and he often felt useless and bored. When he was not moved by guilt to find himself something to do, Ayer enjoyed himself thoroughly, visiting friends, dancing, drinking, meeting women. He wrote to Renée from New York, asking her to join him there, but she turned down the invitation and announced that she wanted a divorce. He began an affair with Sheilah Graham, who had formerly been a showgirl, a Hollywood gossip columnist, and a lover of F. Scott Fitzgerald. (Graham's daughter, Wendy Fairey, found out at age 46 that Ayer was her father.[31]) He apparently did not succeed quite so well at wooing another woman he dated briefly, known then as Betty (later Lauren) Bacall.

In 1943, Ayer returned to England, then was posted to Accra in the Gold Coast (now Ghana), but was recalled almost immediately, apparently because he made it clear to everyone how stupid and useless he thought the British army operations there were. His next posting was to France, where he was to monitor and analyze political developments as the war drew to a close. As usual, he managed to combine his army duties with a good deal of socializing.

Back to Philosophy

When Ayer returned from the war, he and Renée lived together for a while, but then separated and divorced. To his dismay, Ayer found that he had to cite Hampshire as corespondent in the divorce; this effectively killed Hampshire's prospects for a future career at stuffy Victorian Oxford.

Ayer found that the post-war Oxford philosophical climate had undergone a drastic change:

---

[30] *PML* 233.
[31] Fairey has published her memoirs: *One of the Family* (New York: W. W. Norton & Company, 1992).

My own views, which had been thought so revolutionary before the war, were now regarded not merely as orthodox but even as old-fashioned. I had mysteriously passed from being a young Turk to being, at the age of thirty-five, almost an elder statesman, without ever having known the plenitude of office.[32]

Ryle was still the major philosophical influence at Oxford, but J. L. Austin's reputation was growing, and by the fifties Austin's "ordinary language" methodology had become thought of as the Oxford philosophy. Ayer thought that this brand of philosophy was of little use, and did not like Austin very much.

It was characteristic of Austin that he was the only one of us whom the rest never called by his Christian name. He was not unfriendly, but his friendliness was impersonal.... He had high moral principles and a quiet self-confidence which many people found intimidating. I respected him for his character and his intelligence but never made the effort, which would almost certainly have been fruitless, to get to know him more intimately.[33]

The second edition of *LTL*, for which Ayer had prepared a new introduction, appeared in 1946. In the introduction, Ayer clarified some of his earlier views and amended or retracted others. Sales of the book continued to rise, and reached enormous levels with the appearance of a paperback edition in 1952. All his later work circled around substantially the same issues he had dealt with in *LTL*; but it was more careful, often more tentative and less doctrinaire. It was less exciting but more believable—at least, to mature philosophers, if not to the impressionable beginning students who formed an important proportion of *LTL*'s readership.

In later years, Ayer regretted the fact that he was famous almost entirely on the basis of *LTL*:

Language, Truth and Logic made my name as a philosopher and I am gratified by its continued success. What sometimes annoys me is to find it is still rated above all my later work. I should prefer to think that I had made some progress in the course of the past forty years.[34]

---

[32] *PML* 294-5.
[33] *PML* 161.
[34] *PML* 299.

In 1946, at the age of 35, Ayer was elected to the professorship in philosophy at University College, London. When Ayer arrived there, he found that the Philosophy Department was in two tiny rooms in one of the outlying and more dilapidated parts of the college. There were half a dozen or so undergraduate philosophy students, no graduate students, only one qualified teacher, no secretary, and no telephone. Ayer got to work on improving the department. He hired Stuart Hampshire (motivated, perhaps, by the guilt he felt for having ruined Hampshire's Oxford career), then Richard Wollheim; he procured some graduate students for the department, and even a telephone. By the time he left thirteen years later, it had grown from the "shambles" it had been when he arrived into a major philosophy department, but one quite different in spirit from the Oxbridge departments: this one was enthusiastic, freewheeling, left-wing, avant-garde, anti-establishment, and strongly analytic.

Radio and Television

Ayer's media appearances began during the late forties, and by the beginning of the sixties he had become something of a celebrity, mostly because of his frequent participation on a BBC television program called "Brains Trust," a talk show involving academics, scientists, writers, and entertainers. Ayer's wide cultural knowledge and his enormous skill at amusing intelligent off-the-cuff talk made him a star, outstanding even among Britain's extraordinarily glib chattering classes.

One could also see him on TV discussing professional soccer, a topic of continuing passionate interest for him. (A close friend recalls that the only time she saw him genuinely upset was when seven members of the Manchester United soccer team were killed in a plane crash.[35]) Ayer suspected that his attraction as a sports commentator was due less to his expertise than to the oddity of the appearance of a learned academic philosopher as soccer fanatic.

But his media experience was not always a success. A memorable BBC television broadcast involved Ayer and the sexy pop singer Eartha Kitt in a discussion of romantic love. While he "tried to talk learnedly about the troubadors,"[36] Eartha Kitt's hand could be seen on screen, stroking his neck and playing with his ear. "Oooh, tell us about love,

---

[35] Rogers 251.
[36] A. J. Ayer, *More of My Life* (London: Collins, 1985) 145. This second volume of Ayer's autobiography will be referred to as *MML*.

prof baby!" crooned Kitt. Ayer reports "I floundered on and was made to look thoroughly foolish."[37]

Ayer was a perennial traveler. His memoirs record his visits to almost every European country, the U.S., Canada, and Mexico, the Gold Coast (Ghana), Morocco and Algeria, Peru, Uruguay, and Brazil, Russia, China, India, Pakistan, and Israel.

But he did find the time during the early fifties to write several articles and his next book, *The Problem of Knowledge*.[38] Ayer thought that this was his best book to date, more original and better-worked out, and his critics mostly agreed. It reexamines the topics Ayer had been dealing with throughout his career, but this time with the central theme of answering skepticism about our knowledge of physical objects, the past and future, other minds, and personal identity.

Ayer was an extraordinarily prolific writer. His lifetime output includes thirteen books of philosophy, five collections of his essays, three anthologies of others' works, two volumes of autobiography, just under 300 published essays, and innumerable letters-to-the-editor.

Oxford Again

In 1959 Ayer moved back to Oxford, as the Wykeham Professor of Logic. He lists as his motives for the move that this new job offered a good deal of prestige, a challenge that he thought he needed, and the opportunity to combat the dominant influence there of Wittgenstein and Austin. Ryle wrote Ayer a welcome letter confessing that he had voted against him for the chair. Austin, who also voted against him, did not write. Austin died shortly after Ayer took up the chair, but his posthumously published book *Sense and Sensibilia*,[39] an extended attack on Ayer's views on perception, continued the battle beyond the grave.

During the fifties, Ayer and his ex-wife saw each other frequently, on an affectionate basis, while he continued his active and promiscuous social life. Beginning around 1957, his main (though not exclusive) lover was an American woman, Dee Wells ("loud, glamorous, and very funny in a tough-talking way..., her 'mother-fuckers' dropped, in a deep bourbon drawl."[40]) They were married in 1960.

---

[37] *MML* 145.

[38] (London: Macmillan, 1956). This will be referred to as *PK*.

[39] (Oxford: Oxford UP, 1962).

[40] Rogers 245.

The Sixties

In Dee's view,

> Freddie was at his very best in the early Sixties, very upright
> and open-minded. He was happy in himself and fair. He was
> certainly the nicest man in the world.[41]

But this from Stuart Hampshire:

> From being a man of the Left, he became Establishment. From
> being anti-club he joined them and was always having lunch at
> the French Embassy. He came to see himself as an important
> cultural figure. He is almost the only person whom I have ever
> known who really changed. Gaiety and heterodoxy gave way
> to self-consciousness. From my point of view it was down-
> hill.[42]

Ayer had become more "establishment," but his political views remained what they had always been: left-liberal, not radical. During the
sixties, he became involved in a large number of high-profile commit-
tees agitating for liberal law reform on abortion and homosexuality, and
against racial discrimination and the Vietnam War. He wrote countless
letters-to-editors. To the dismay of the more radically minded, he was
given a knighthood in 1970, and tended thereafter to give his name as
'Professor Sir Alfred Ayer'. He was becoming a bit pompous.

In 1968, he published *The Origins of Pragmatism*,[43] a book that
seemed to please no one. Four more books followed during the next
five years: *Russell and Moore: The Analytical Heritage*,[44] *Probability
and Evidence*,[45] *Russell*,[46] and *The Central Questions of Philosophy*.[47]
A major concern in the *Probability* book was the problem of induction;
Ayer took the Humean line that it could not be justified without circu-
larity. The *Central Questions* book was intended as a successor to Russell's best-selling introductory work *The Problems of Philosophy* published in 1912. Like Russell, Ayer takes on skepticism; he argues here

---

[41] Rogers 278.
[42] Rogers 260.
[43] (London: Macmillan, 1968).
[44] (London: Macmillan, 1971).
[45] (London: Macmillan, 1972).
[46] (London: Fontana, 1972).
[47] (London: Weidenfeld & Nicolson, 1973). This book will be referred
to below as *CQP*.

that the external world and other minds are not directly perceived, but are posited as the best explanations for our perceptual experience.

Following this burst of publication, there was a lull in Ayer's philosophical work, though he lectured, wrote popular articles, and produced the first of his two volumes of autobiography. The autobiographical works are peculiar. They record a large number of incidents in great detail—Ayer had a phenomenal memory—but very little in the way of insight or analysis of others or of himself. A New York Times reviewer wrote that the first book was "vain" and "arctic"; "all fact and no feeling."[48] Ayer's biographer judges that "the book has no center," appropriately, he thinks, for an author who endorsed Hume's view of the self as a substance-less bundle of perceptions.[49]

Retirement and Old Age

Ayer retired from Oxford in 1978, but took on a visiting professorship at Surrey. Several books followed: *Hume,*[50] *Philosophy in the Twentieth Century,*[51] *Wittgenstein,*[52] *Voltaire,*[53] and *Thomas Paine.*[54] The Wittgenstein book was respectful but highly critical. The Voltaire and Paine books, Ayer admitted, both suffered a bit from lack of scholarship, and neither gave much insight into the personality of their subject; but both of them did attract interest as serious treatments of historical radical thinkers by a contemporary one.

His marriage had become stormy and distant, and both he and Dee (having agreed on an "open marriage") were deeply involved in affairs. They separated in 1979, and Ayer moved in with Vanessa Lawson, who was twenty-six years younger than he, and whom he married in 1982, immediately following his divorce from Dee. They were devoted to each other, and Ayer, for once, was monogamous.

His daughter Valerie died in 1981, and his wife Vanessa in 1985, and both events left him deeply shaken. Friends recalled the rare event of Ayer's showing his feelings.

---

[48] John Sturrock, review of *PML* in *New York Times Book Review* 22 January 1978; quoted in Rogers 315.

[49] Rogers 315.

[50] (Oxford: Oxford UP, 1980).

[51] (London: Weidenfeld & Nicolson, 1981).

[52] (London: Weidenfeld & Nicolson, 1985).

[53] (London: Weidenfeld & Nicolson, 1986).

[54] (London: Seker & Warburg, 1989).

He was clearly getting old, but still demonstrated a good deal of his former vitality and fearlessness. At age 77, he was attending a fashionable party in New York, chatting to a group of young models and fashion designers, when a woman rushed up, saying that a friend was being assaulted in the bedroom. Ayer went to investigate, and found Mike Tyson forcing himself on Naomi Campbell (the future super-model). Ayer warned Tyson to stop. Tyson said, "Do you know who the fuck I am? I'm the heavyweight champion of the world." Ayer replied, "And I am the former Wykeham Professor of Logic. We are both pre-eminent in our field; I suggest that we talk about this like rational men." They began to talk, while Naomi Campbell slipped out.[55]

Ayer's Life After Death

In June 1988, during a bout of pneumonia, Ayer's heart stopped for four minutes before he was revived. Later on, recalling his experiences during these four minutes, he wrote:

> I was confronted by a red light, exceedingly bright, and also very painful even when I turned away from it. I was aware that this light was responsible for the government of the universe. Among its ministers were two creatures who had been put in charge of space. These ministers periodically inspected space and had recently carried out such an inspection. They had, however, failed to do their work properly, with the result that space, like a badly fitting jigsaw puzzle, was slightly out of joint. A further consequence was that the laws of nature had ceased to function as they should. I felt that it was up to me to put things right.[56]

Ayer admits that this experience might be delusive, but cites a report of someone else who suffered a heart stoppage and also saw a bright red light; this, he says, is a "slight indication that it [his own experience] might have been veridical.... On the face of it, these experiences...are rather strong evidence that death does not put an end to consciousness."[57] He insists that the existence of an after-life does not imply the existence of God, but:

---

[55] Rogers 344.

[56] "What I Saw When I was Dead...," London Sunday *Telegraph*, 28 August 1988; reprinted as "Still More of My Life" in Hahn 46.

[57] "What I Saw..." 47.

It is conceivable that one's experiences in the next world, if there are any, will supply evidence of a god's existence, but we have no right to presume on such evidence, when we have not had the relevant experience.[58]

In a follow-up article he said that he was still firmly an atheist, and still believed that death would be the end of him, but admitted that his experiences had weakened his "inflexible attitude" and had led him to think that the question of survival was worth philosophical consideration.[59] This represented a reversal of his earlier view that the question of an after-life was either metaphysical and meaningless, or self-contradictory because of the analytic criteria of personal identity through time. Even more extraordinarily, he appeared now to regard God's existence as possibly verifiable.

Ayer's death and resurrection also appeared to have an emotional effect. Friends reported that he began to enjoy life more. Dee said, "Freddie has got so much nicer since he died."[60] He resumed his writing and his flirtations, and remarried Dee in April 1989. In the middle of June, he was back in the hospital. He knew he was dying, but remained determinedly calm and cheerful.

---

[58] "What I Saw" 48.

[59] "Postscript to a Postmortem," (London) *Spectator* 15, October 1988; reprinted in "Still More of My Life" 50.

[60] Rogers 349.

3

Meaning and Verification

The Central Thesis of *LTL*

Ayer presented the central thesis of *Language, Truth and Logic* in the first paragraph of the Preface to its First Edition:

> Like Hume, I divide all genuine propositions into two classes: those which, in his terminology, concern "relations of ideas," and those which concern "matters of fact." The former class comprises the *a priori* propositions of logic and pure mathematics, and these I allow to be necessary and certain only because they are analytic. That is, I maintain that the reason why these propositions cannot be confuted in experience is that they do not make any assertion about the empirical world, but simply record our determination to use symbols in a certain fashion. Propositions concerning empirical matters of fact, on the other hand, I hold to be hypotheses, which can be probable but never certain.... To test whether a sentence expresses a genuine empirical hypothesis ... I require ...that some possible sense-experience should be relevant to the determination of its truth or falsehood. If a putative proposition fails to satisfy this principle, and is not a tautology, then I hold that it is metaphysical, and that, being metaphysical, it is neither true nor false but literally senseless. It will be found that much of what ordinarily passes for philosophy is metaphysical according to this criterion.[1]

---

[1] *LTL* 31.

The last two sentences of this quote are the bombshell Ayer hurled into the philosophical community: his advice that one should toss much of past philosophy into the garbage heap. We can imagine his gleeful anticipation of the horrified reaction from the philosophical old guard.

Some Distinctions

It will be helpful in discussing Ayer's central position to begin by reviewing some basic philosophical distinctions that are relevant here, and some history of the debate over the issue.

Distinction 1: Analytic/Synthetic

These terms were introduced by Kant to refer to two kinds of *judgment*; but nowadays, philosophers usually prefer to use this to distinguish two kinds of (indicative and meaningful) *sentences*: a sentence is analytic when its truth (or falsity) depends entirely on the meanings of the symbols involved, otherwise synthetic.

Ayer gives this uncontroversial example of an analytic sentence: 'Every oculist is an eye-doctor.'[2] The truth of this sentence is wholly a consequence of the fact that the term 'oculist' is synonymous with the term 'eye-doctor' (plus, of course, the logical form given by the rest of the sentence). Similarly, 'Every bachelor is unmarried' is analytic; its truth follows from the meanings of 'bachelor' and of 'unmarried.' (These symbols are not synonymous; but 'bachelor' is synonymous with 'unmarried man,' so we might say that the meaning of 'bachelor' "contains" the meaning of 'unmarried.') We say that both of these sentences are "true by definition."

Other analytic sentences are those whose truth or falsity depends wholly on their logical form; we might want to say that these are true (or false) by definition of their logical words. "All bachelors are bachelors" is an example of this. "It is Thursday or it is not Thursday" is another. This sort of analytic sentence is what is sometimes loosely called a "tautology." The negation of these logically true sentences is (or leads to) a logical self-contradiction.

Distinction 2: A priori/A posteriori

This distinction concerns how something can be *known* to be true (or false). It can be known a priori if it can be known before, or independently of, sense experience of the fact in question, or of evidence

---

[2] *LTL* 85.

for the fact. When empirical observation or evidence is necessary for knowing something, then it is said to be a posteriori.

One can know that all oculists are eye-doctors without having to observe even one oculist, and without having to collect any empirical evidence. In this case, it is clear how this a priori knowledge is possible. Once one understands the meanings of the words, one can know that the sentence is true, because it is analytic. So it is no mystery that, and why, analytic truths are knowable a priori. But it is philosophically controversial whether any synthetic truths are knowable a priori.

Distinction 3: Necessary/Contingent

Something is a necessary truth when it could not have been otherwise. Contingent truths are those that could have been otherwise. Usually philosophers take these '*could*'s in a peculiarly strong sense. In this sense, it "could" be the case that pigs fly, despite the fact that they are grounded by their anatomy and the laws of aerodynamics. In the sense of 'possible' involved here, we might imagine a possible world in which the laws of aerodynamics were entirely different, or a possible world in which pigs had wings and a much more birdlike shape and size; so in this sense, it is possible (but actually false, of course) that pigs fly. So 'Pigs do not fly' is contingent.

What then is necessary? Analytic truths provide clear and uncontroversial examples of necessary truths. It is not only true that oculists are eye-doctors—it is necessarily true. It would be impossible for anybody simultaneously to be an oculist but not an eye-doctor—by definition, of course. And logical truths are necessary as well. The statement "It is raining or it is not raining" is true here now, and at every other time and place, and it *must* be true.

Again, there is a controversy here, on the question whether there are any synthetic truths that are necessary.

A Little History

In the quote at the beginning of this chapter, Ayer refers to the distinction made by the great eighteenth-century British philosopher David Hume between "relations of ideas" and "matters of fact."[3] Rela-

---

[3] This distinction is introduced at the beginning of Section IV of Hume's *An Enquiry Concerning Human Understanding* (1748). It does not occur—in these terms—in Hume's other major work, *A Treatise of Human Nature* (1738), though what he says there can be interpreted to be roughly equivalent.

tion-of-ideas propositions, Hume says, are "discoverable by the mere operation of thought" (they are a priori). Matters of fact "are not ascertained in the same manner" (they are a posteriori). "The contrary of every matter of fact is still possible" (matters of fact are contingent) but relations-of-ideas propositions are necessary; their contrary implies a "contradiction" (they are analytic). Hume can be taken to be claiming here that the only source for the necessity of any proposition is that it is analytic; and that the only propositions that can be known a priori are the analytic ones. This is the denial of the existence of any synthetic but necessary propositions, and of any that are synthetic and a priori.

Interpreted this way, Hume's positions are exactly identical to the ones Ayer expressed, crediting Hume, in *LTL*. A close and careful reading of Hume, however, raises doubts that Hume really is making exactly these claims. But we shall ignore this; what is important to us is not what Hume really meant, but what he was taken to be claiming by most philosophers, including Ayer.

The denial of the existence of any synthetic a priori knowledge, generally taken to be one of the tenets at the very core of empiricism, conflicted with a good deal of what philosophers have had to say before and after Hume. Notoriously, it appeared to rule out the possibility of knowledge of many philosophical pronouncements—those which were neither analytic (that is, in Hume's terms, did not contain "abstract reasoning concerning quantity or number"), and were not empirically confirmable (in Hume's terms, were not the result of "experimental reasoning concerning matter of fact and existence"). Hume famously wrote:

> When we run over libraries, persuaded of these principles, what havoc must we make? If we take in our hand any volume; of divinity or school metaphysics, for instance; let us ask, *Does it contain any abstract reasoning concerning quantity or number?* No. *Does it contain any experimental reasoning concerning matter of fact and existence?* No. Commit it then to the flames: for it can contain nothing but sophistry and illusion.[4]

Hume can be taken to be claiming here that synthetic assertions are worthless if disconnected from any "experimental reasoning"—that is, if not associated with possible experience that would verify (or falsify) them. A synthetic claim that has not in fact been verified by experience cannot be knowledge; but the problem Hume is pointing to is that cer-

---

[4] *Enquiry*, Sect. XII, Part III.

tain synthetic statements "of divinity or school metaphysics" cannot possibly be verified by experience, because they are not associated with any possible experiences that would verify them. So Hume's claim is that spoken or written sentences are worthless nonsense if they are not associated with genuine ideas—that is, if they are not capable of perceptual verification.

Very early on in his philosophical development, Ayer found this view in Hume:

> In a comment on Hume's method which I wrote on the fly-leaf of my copy of *A Treatise of Human Nature*, when I first read this work as an undergraduate, I concluded by saying: 'In order to discover what he means, he studies the phenomena by which his proposition is verified.'[5]

Immanuel Kant (1724-1804) agreed with Hume that some "speculative metaphysics" went beyond our capacity for knowledge; but he disagreed with Hume about the synthetic a priori. For example, he agreed with Hume that arithmetic and geometry were constituted by necessary and a priori statements, but argued that they were synthetic. Another example of what Kant thought was synthetic, but necessary and a priori, was the proposition, 'Every event has a cause.'

Later empiricists accepted Hume's rejection of the synthetic necessary a priori, but differed in various small ways. Ayer (as we shall see) agreed with Hume that arithmetic and geometry were necessary, a priori, and analytic; John Stuart Mill, however, argued that they were synthetic, contingent, and a posteriori.

The Vienna Circle saw itself as continuing in the footsteps of Hume. Members of the Circle disagreed occasionally about various matters, but according to Ayer, they generally agreed that logical and mathematical truths were "tautologies, owing their necessity to linguistic conventions,"[6] and that any synthetic sentence "that could not be empirically verified was literally nonsensical; this included most of what went under the name of metaphysics or theology."[7]

Clearly the Vienna Circle was a source for many of Ayer's *LTL* views; another source was the Cambridge philosophers: Russell, C. D. Broad, G. E. Moore, and the early Wittgenstein. Russell's empiricism was a general influence on Ayer, but he took Wittgenstein's work to establish *LTL*'s central thesis:

---

[5] *PML* 116.
[6] "MMD" 16.
[7] "MMD" 16-17.

> Significant propositions, I learned from [Wittgenstein's]
> *Tractatus*, fell into two classes: either they were tautologies,
> like the propositions of logic and pure mathematics, or they
> were empirically verifiable. Everything else, including meta-
> physics and theology, was literally nonsensical.[8]

Wittgenstein and the Vienna Circle were not independent sources for
these similar views. Wittgenstein had participated in the Circle, and
they agreed with Ayer about what was to be learned from the *Tractatus*.
But most other interpreters of Wittgenstein have thought that this attri-
bution was a mistake. About this matter of interpretation, Ayer says:

> I took it for granted that the 'atomic propositions' which
> served in the *Tractatus* to determine the sense of everything
> that could be said, were propositions which referred to observ-
> able states of affairs. This was not made explicit by Wittgen-
> stein himself, and is now thought by some of his disciples not
> to have been what he intended, but it was an assumption gen-
> erally made at the time by those who latched on to the *Trac-
> tatus*, including philosophers with whom Wittgenstein was
> personally in contact. If he did not accept it, one wonders why
> he allowed them to think that he did. Whether he accepted it or
> not, it was an assumption that suited the positivism which his
> Viennese followers had inherited and one that also fitted the
> *Tractatus* into the tradition of British empiricism.[9]

Ayer, incidentally, found that attributing positions to Wittgenstein was
dangerous:

> I knew from the experiences of others that one had to be very
> careful in what one said about him if he was not to take of-
> fence. In particular, he had displayed a tendency to denounce
> any reference to his current views either as plagiarism or as
> misrepresentation.[10]

The Verification Principle

This is Ayer's statement of the verification principle of meaningfulness:

> We say that a sentence is factually significant to any given
> person, if, and only if, he knows how to verify the proposition

---

[8] *PML* 115-6.
[9] *PML* 116.
[10] *PML* 304.

which it purports to express—that is, if he knows what observations would lead him, under certain conditions, to accept the proposition as being true, or reject it as being false. If, on the other hand, the putative proposition is of such a character that the assumption of its truth, or falsehood, is consistent with any assumption whatsoever concerning the nature of his future experience, then, as far as he is concerned, it is, if not a tautology, a mere pseudo-proposition.[11]

It should be noted that when Ayer uses the word 'verify,' he usually means *verify or falsify*.

Verification and Meaning

Often it was not made clear by Ayer or the Vienna Circle philosophers whether the verification principle was intended merely as the test whether or not a sentence had meaning, or in addition as indicating what constituted the meaning of any meaningful sentence. Interpreted the first way, the principle claims that the only (non-analytic) statements that are factually meaningful are those with associated with verification sense-experiences. Interpreted the second way, it claims that the meaning of any meaningful (non-analytic) statement is given by its associated verification sense-experiences. The second view entails the first: if the meaning of any meaningful sentence is constituted by its association with verifying sense-experiences, then a sentence with no associated verifying sense-experiences would be meaningless.

The second view is more radical than the first. Certain statements are clearly and directly about experiences (the ones which express what Ayer calls "experiential propositions"), for example, 'I'm having a red experience'; but most ordinary ones are not, on the face of things, about experience at all. The sentence 'There is a red apple in front of me now' appears to be about an apple, not about anyone's experience of an apple. Apple-experiences verify the apple-statement, but they do not appear to be what the statement says, to give its meaning. So the second claim seems highly implausible.

But empiricists sometimes have felt themselves to be driven into this implausible position. The general argument here is based on the premise, accepted by all empiricists, that knowledge of any genuine fact arises from our sense-experience. So the propositions we know must be limited to those which describe the content of our experience. But clearly we can know propositions which assert the existence of

---

[11] *LTL* 35.

"external objects" such as apple. So those propositions—and any propositions expressing genuine facts we are capable of knowing—must really be about the content of our experience. Thus these propositions might be translatable into statements explicitly about sense-experience. Clearly things exist unperceived; so, for example, that apple could exist even inside the closed refrigerator, when no corresponding experience propositions are true. So translation should be done into actual *or possible* experiences: If someone were to open the fridge, then that person would have a red-experience.

This position is called *phenomenalism*, and Ayer argues for it in *LTL*:

> We know that it must be possible to define material things in terms of sense-contents, because it is only by the occurrence of certain sense-contents that the existence of any material thing can ever be in the least degree verified. And thus we see that we have not to enquire whether a phenomenalist "theory of perception" or some other sort of theory is correct, but only what form of phenomenalist theory is correct.[12]

Some Difficulties

Sometimes a perfectly meaningful proposition has not in fact been verified by anyone—nobody has had any of the experiences which give its meaning. Ayer points out that in some cases a proposition has not been verified merely because we have not taken the trouble to do so; and in others, we could not verify the proposition even if we chose to, "simply because we lack the practical means of placing ourselves in the situation where the relevant observations could be made."[13] He gives Schlick's example of one such proposition: that there are mountains on the far side of the moon. Were we able to travel by rocket to the far side of the moon (and then, of course, we were not), we would have experiences that would show that this proposition is true or false. The fact that we do associate such conceivable (though not practically obtainable) experiences with this proposition shows that it is a meaningful factual proposition.

By contrast, Ayer displays this sentence: "The Absolute enters into, but is itself incapable of, evolution and progress." There are, Ayer claims, no conceivable observations that would be relevant to the truth or falsity of this sentence. He adds that this sentence would mean

---

[12] *LTL* 53.
[13] *LTL* 36.

something if its speaker were using the words with some meaning different from their conventional English meaning, and, with this unconventional meaning, the sentence were associated with verifying experiences (or were analytic). But given the conventional English reading of this sentence, it is literally nonsense: the speaker "has made an utterance which has no literal significance even for himself."[14]

Ayer calls a meaningful non-analytic physical-object assertion a *factual proposition*, and one that "records an actual or possible observation" an *experiential proposition*. Phenomenalists claim that factual (non-analytic, physical-object statements) are really about sense-experiences; so each factual statement can be analyzed—translated—into experiential propositions. Ayer calls the relation between the factual proposition and the experiential propositions into which it can be translated "equivalence." To say that two sentences **P** and **Q** are equivalent is to say that that **P** and **Q** are interdeducible, that is that **P** implies **Q**, and **Q** implies **P**.

It is clear that a typical factual proposition is not equivalent to any single experiential proposition. Consider the factual proposition

FP: There is a red apple here now.

We would associate the truth of this statement with the presence of a red visual experience on the part of the observer, that is, with the experiential proposition

EP: I am having a red experience.

And we would count this red-experience as (at least partially) verifying **FP**. But if **EP** translates **FP** at all, it provides only a partial translation. There are all sorts of other experiences verifying the presence of the apple: its smell, its feel, its taste, visual impressions of its shape and size, and so on. Furthermore, slight changes in the conditions of sensing produce different experiences. Changes in the color of illumination, for example, produce visual experiences of different colors; and moving around the apple, or further or closer to it, produce different visual appearances. And there are indefinitely many relevant different conditions and resulting different experiences. Perhaps a full translation of **FP** could not be accomplished with a finite number of experiential propositions; in any case, it would be larger than could be achieved in practice.

Another difficulty that phenomenalists are well aware of was the problem of illusion and hallucination. When this happens, experiential

---

[14] *LTL* 36.

propositions are true, but the associated factual statement is false. For example, if I hallucinate an apple before me, I might have any number of appropriate apple-experiences, but no apple is there. This is a problem for the phenomenalist because the experiential propositions do not entail the factual propositions, so equivalence fails.

Attempting to accommodate all these matters, Ayer says that his claim is not that each genuine factual proposition should be equivalent to an experiential proposition, or any finite number of experiential propositions. His position regarding the logical relation between factual and experiential propositions is this: Each genuinely factual proposition is such that

> some experiential propositions can be deduced from it in conjunction with certain other premises without being deducible from those other premises alone.[15]

So, for example, the experiential proposition

EP: I'm having a red experience now.

is supposed to be deducible from the factual proposition

FP: There is a red apple in front of me now.

plus "certain other premises," the ones we might call condition-propositions, stating certain conditions of observation, which would result in this sort of experience. The presence of a red apple in front of me would not imply that I am having a red experience, because if my eyes were closed while that red apple were there, I wouldn't have that experience. So in order to deduce **EP**, we would need to add to **FP** the condition-proposition

CP1: My eyes are open.

But this would not do, because even if my eyes were open, I would not have a red experience if the apple were not in my line of sight—that is, if there were something opaque between me and the apple. So we should have to add

CP2: The apple is in my line of sight.

But of course it is easy to think of other conditions that must be in place also, for example, that the light shining on the apple is white, that I am not color-blind, that I do not have severe cataracts in my eyes, that I am conscious, and on and on.

It seems, then, that enumerating all the necessary additional premises to make **EP** deducible from **FP** would be impossible. Perhaps we

---

[15] *LTL* 39.

might find it satisfactory instead to just add to **FP** the general vague statement that conditions for observation were "normal," whatever that means, exactly.

We can see why Ayer specified that the **EP** not be deducible from the additional premises alone. This condition is necessary because otherwise every sentence would turn out to express a genuinely factual proposition. Consider, for example, Ayer's own example of a nonsense statement

NS: The Absolute enters into, but is itself incapable of, evolution and progress.

From **NS** plus this auxiliary premise:

AP1: I'm having a red experience and the sky is blue.

one can deduce

EP: I'm having a red experience.

In this case, **NS** adds nothing to the deduction: **EP** is deducible from **AP1** alone. So Ayer adds that the **EP** must not be deducible from the other, auxiliary premises alone.

But this will not do either, as Ayer realized after *LTL* was published. Note that from the nonsense statement

NS: The Absolute enters into, but is itself incapable of, evolution and progress.

plus this auxiliary premise:

AP2: If the Absolute enters into, but is itself incapable of, evolution and progress, then I'm having a red experience.

one can deduce

EP: I'm having a red experience.

and **EP** cannot be deduced from the auxiliary premise alone. So this is a clear counter-example to Ayer's criterion. The problem is that Ayer has not imposed any restrictions on what sort of auxiliary premise is allowable.

Ayer attempted to patch things up in the Introduction to the Second Edition, by amending his criterion, restricting the auxiliary premises in a complicated way, which we won't go into here. But it turned out that his restriction did not do the job either. Philosophical debate continues about whether this problem can be solved.[16]

---

[16] For a reasonably clear account—as clear, anyway, as the logical complexities here admit—of the problems and further attempts at solu-

Meaning and Evidence

Having an experience in the set associated with a factual proposition verifies—gives evidence for—that factual proposition, but it is not the case that every experience that gives evidence for a factual statement is a part of the set that gives that proposition's meaning. Ayer demonstrates this using the following example:

> The statement that I have blood on my coat may, in certain circumstances, confirm the hypothesis that I have committed a murder, but it is not part of the meaning of the statement that I have committed a murder that I should have blood upon my coat, nor, as I understand it, does the principle of verification imply that it is.[17]

Ayer must then distinguish between evidence for **P** that gives part of the meaning of **P**, and evidence for **P** that does not.

When, then, is evidence for **P** a genuine verification condition for **P**, and part of its meaning? Here is Ayer's answer:

> One statement may be evidence for another, and still neither itself express a necessary condition of the truth of this other statement, nor belong to any set of statements which determines a range within such a necessary condition falls; and it is only in these cases that the principle of verification yields the conclusion that the one statement is part of the meaning of the other.

The blood on Fred's coat is evidence for the truth of 'Fred did the murder,' but it is not a necessary condition for its truth. 'Fred did the murder' might be true even though there is no blood on his coat. Neither is the blood on Fred's coat one of a (finite) set of conditions { **C1, C2, C3**... } such that the obtaining of at least one of these conditions is necessary.

But this will not do to distinguish evidence that is part of meaning from evidence that is not. Consider this example: Suppose that when Fred eats toast for breakfast, he invariably leaves crumbs on the table; and this is the only possible reason why those crumbs are there. So the presence of crumbs on the table is (conclusive) evidence that Fred ate toast for breakfast. 'There are crumbs on the table' is a necessary con-

---

tion, see John Foster, *Ayer* (London: Routledge & Kegan Paul, 1985) 14ff.

[17] *LTL* 14.

dition for the truth of 'Fred ate toast for breakfast.' But the first statement does not give part of the meaning of the second.

What Ayer needs here is a way to distinguish cases when a statement **E** is merely evidence for **P** from cases in which **E** constitutes a partial specification of the meaning of **P**. The fact that **E** is necessary for **P** does not do this. He should have said that **E** was necessary for **S** because of the meanings of the words involved; that is, that (roughly speaking) 'If **P** then **E**' was analytic. Thus, for example, suppose that my having a red-experience (under certain conditions) is not merely evidence for the truth of the sentence, 'There is a red thing in front of me'; suppose that it is (at least) part of the meaning of that sentence. Then 'If there is a red thing in front of me, then (under certain conditions) I have a red experience' is analytically true. The analytic truth of this would be a consequence of the fact that (at least part of) the *meaning* of 'There is a red thing in front of me' is '(Under certain conditions) I have a red experience.'

This solution is implicit in Ayer's discussion of the following objection. 'God exists' is a sentence that Ayer judges to be devoid of factual content. (We shall look at his views on religion later.) But, as he is aware, some religious believers contend that there is empirical evidence for this claim: "It is sometimes claimed, indeed, that the existence of a certain sort of regularity in nature constitutes sufficient evidence for the existence of a god."[18] The word 'sufficient' in here is not important. If there is any empirical evidence for the existence of God, sufficient or insufficient—indeed, if it is even conceivable what evidence for or against God's existence would be like, even though none actually existed on either side of this question—then it seems that Ayer should have to admit that the sentence does have factual content, and is capable of being true or false.

Ayer's response to this argument is:

> If the sentence "God exists" entails no more than that certain types of phenomena occur in certain sequences, then to assert the existence of a god will be simply equivalent to asserting that there is the requisite regularity in nature; and no religious man would admit that this was all he intended to assert in asserting the existence of a god.[19]

Ayer is here arguing, in effect, that if this were all the religious person meant by 'God exists,' then Ayer would be happy to admit that that

---

[18] *LTL* 115.
[19] *LTL* 115.

person's utterance was meaningful and indeed true. But this is not what religious people intend—mean—by such utterances.

For Ayer, to determine the meaning of 'God exists' we should investigate not merely what people would take as evidence for it. The fact that someone would take certain sorts of order in the universe as evidence for the existence of God is not relevant, unless this fact constituted part of the meaning of 'God exists'—in other words, unless it were "true by definition" that if God exists, then there are certain sorts of order in the universe. But (Ayer's argument could continue) people do not take this to be a consequence of the definition of the terms involved. In other words, this evidence does not constitute a partial specification of the meaning of the assertion 'God exists.' Failing the existence of any other verification conditions—i.e., of evidence that is an analytic consequence of the meaning of the sentence 'God exists,' we can conclude that this sentence is without descriptive meaning.

You may have been thinking that the way this distinction has been stated makes no real progress. We have distinguished empirical evidence for **P** that constitutes a (partial) meaning specification for **P** from empirical evidence for **P** that does not, on the basis of what follows analytically from **P**. But this gets us no further; for to say that something follows analytically from **P** is merely to say that it is a consequence of what **P** means. Are we locked into a circle here? In the next chapter, we shall consider an influential objection to Ayer's position by W. V. Quine, which argues that there is no non-circular way to make the distinction between meaning-specification and mere evidence.

Meaning and Equivalence

Ayer's claim is that every meaningful factual statement is equivalent to a set of experience statements. That means that the factual statement is true if and only if the set of experience statements is true. But does it follow that the factual statement's *meaning* is given by the set of experience statements?

Ayer admits that, in a sense, it does not.

> I think that if we are to use the sign "meaning" in the way in which it is most commonly used, we must not say that two sentences have the same meaning for anyone, unless the occurrence of one always has the same effect on his thoughts and actions as the occurrence of the other. And, clearly, it is possible for two sentences to be equivalent, by our criterion, without having the same effect on anyone who employs the language.

33

So two equivalent statements might differ in "meaning" in this larger sense when they have different psychological effects on people. For example, 'Fred is an oculist' might seem to you to have a more dignified and respectful flavor than 'Fred is an eye-doctor'; maybe the first form of words has different associations for you than the second, and arouses different feelings. One might say, then, that the sentences have different "meanings" for you, even though they are analytically equivalent and have exactly the same truth/verification-conditions. In this wider sense of 'meaning,' verification conditions do not give the meaning of factual sentences.

Ayer admits, then, that he is talking about 'meaning' in a special restricted sense, but, he claims, this is an important sense. The verification conditions of a sentence might not exhaust its *psychological meaning*, but they do exhaust what we might call its *cognitive meaning*. Giving the truth/verification conditions of a sentence tell us what must be the case in the world for that sentence to be true, so they tell us what factual commitment people are making about the world when they believe or assert that sentence. A sentence without verification conditions may have all sorts of psychological effects, but because there is nothing that counts as finding out that it is true or false, people who assert or "believe" it are thereby making no commitment about the way the world is.

For Ayer, then, this theoretical list of verification conditions does not give the "meaning" of a statement in a wide sense of 'meaning.' The list does not give the statement's *psychological* content, but it does give its *factual* content.

Ayer suggests that the difference between factual and psychological content explains why people are reluctant to accept the phenomenalism at the core of the verificationist account of meaning:

> The failure of some philosophers to recognize that material things are reducible to sense-contents is very largely due to the fact that no sentence which refers to sense-contents ever has the same psychological effect...as a sentence which refers to a material thing.[20]

A statement without verification conditions may have a good deal of psychological force, but it has no factual content. As we shall see in later chapters, Ayer's application of the verification criterion results in the judgment that a variety of utterances we commonly produce have no "meaning" in the narrower sense of descriptive content. Ayer some-

---

[20] *LTL* 69.

times rather brashly suggests, with Hume, that we therefore condemn such meaningless nonsense to the flames. But in his calmer moments, he is willing to admit that some cognitively meaningless language has other valid functions; and he understands that there is a common use of the word "meaning" which extends more broadly than this function.

4

The A Priori and the Necessary

Empiricism, the A Priori, and the Necessary

In *LTL*, Ayer gives this statement of a problem for empiricists:

> Having admitted that we are empiricists, we must now deal
> with the objection that is commonly brought against all forms
> of empiricism; the objection, namely, that it is impossible on
> empiricist principles to account for our knowledge of neces-
> sary truths. For, as Hume conclusively showed, no general
> proposition whose validity is subject to the test of actual expe-
> rience can ever be logically certain. No matter how often it is
> verified in practice, there still remains the possibility that it
> will be confuted on some future occasion.[1]

Ayer's terminology and reasoning here are not as precise as one might
have liked. He runs together a number of distinctions that should have
been kept separate (see the section called "Some Distinctions," pages
21-2 above). What, for example, does "logically certain" mean? Certainty is an epistemological matter, but the word 'logically' suggests
that he is thinking about analyticity. And what does all this have to do
with necessity? But we can state, with a bit more care to keep things
straight, what Ayer has in mind here.

There are really two traditional problems for empiricists: about the
status of a priori knowledge, and of necessary truths.

---

[1] *LTL* 72.

The Problem of A Priori Knowledge

A central claim of empiricism is (roughly stated) that knowledge can arise only from sense experience: that is, that all knowledge is a posteriori. So empiricists face the problem of knowledge that is apparently a priori: they must claim either that supposed examples of a priori knowledge are, in some sense, not really knowledge of genuine facts at all, or else that the knowledge is really a posteriori.

Kant, who introduced consideration of this problem in its modern form, argued that there was one form of a priori knowledge that should not seem troublesome to anyone: knowledge of analytic propositions. The fact that all eye-doctors are oculists can be known in advance of any empirical investigation into the status of any physicians, because 'All eye-doctors are oculists' is an analytic truth—'eye-doctors' and 'oculists' are synonymous. The meanings of the words guarantee the truth of this sentence.[2] Analyticity thus provides an easy explanation for the fact that this truth can be known a priori: once we know the meanings of those words, we can see that the statement will always turn out true, because anything correctly called 'eye-doctor' would also correctly be called 'oculist.'

But knowledge of analytic propositions, which are true merely by definition, is merely trivial: nothing substantial about the real world is known. In some sense there is no real fact here at all. This sort of a priori knowledge does not trouble the empiricist, who claims that all *substantial* knowledge is a posteriori.

But Kant thought that there were some instances of substantial knowledge, of truths expressible by synthetic sentences, not merely trivially true-by-definition, which could nevertheless be known a priori, the truths of arithmetic and geometry for example. (Kant thought there were additional sorts of synthetic a priori knowledge, but these are the most plausible and most widely-discussed examples he proposed, so we shall deal only with them.)

Empiricists responded to Kant either by arguing that truths of arithmetic and geometry are not a priori (John Stuart Mill's reply) or that they are both analytic (Ayer's). We shall take a close look at both responses.

---

[2] This account of analyticity in terms of the meanings of the words in sentences is not exactly Kant's. We shall have a look at Kant's account shortly.

The Problem of Necessary Truth

The way the distinction between contingent and necessary truths is usually explained is that a contingent truth could have been otherwise, but a necessary truth could not have been. Suppose we take 'No pigs fly' to be contingently true, and '7 + 5 = 12' to be necessarily true. Both sentences, we assume, are fully true—both are perfectly in accord with the genuine fully-obtaining, observable, actual facts of the world. The difference here is supposed to be a matter not of what is *actual*, but of what is *possible*. But if all we can observe is the actual, how could we find out that a flying pig is possible, but not a pile of thirteen things made by adding seven and five? An empiricist, it seems, faces a problem not with knowing that either truth is true—we can observe large numbers of instances of both general truths—but rather with knowing what sort of truth each truth is: that one is necessary and the other contingent.

Analyticity provides an account acceptable to empiricists of some examples of necessity. 'All oculists are eye-doctors' could not be otherwise, because nothing could count as making it false. A counter-instance—an oculist who was not an eye-doctor—would be impossible because the terms 'oculist' and 'eye-doctor' are synonymous.

But this kind of necessity is a trivial matter. A proposition true merely because of the meanings of the words involved says nothing substantial about the world. (This sort of necessity has been called "de dicto" necessity—necessity *about words*—as contrasted with supposedly substantial "de re" necessity—necessity *about things*.)

Kant, however, claimed that arithmetic and geometry were necessary but synthetic. This is the controversial claim.

Mill on Arithmetic and Geometry

Mill's view is that truths of arithmetic and geometry are general factual propositions, established a posteriori, on the basis of experience, and subject to future confutation like all the rest. He argued that geometry, for example, is deductive and necessary only in the sense that its conclusions follow from the premises from which they are deduced. But this sort of reasoning simply retrieves from a general proposition what was previously assumed to be in it, and amounts to no progress in reasoning. The real reasoning takes place in the establishment of the acceptability of these general propositions, which Mill insisted was inductive, a posteriori. The general truth, for example, that two straight lines that intersect do not enclose a surface is something that we know on the basis of the evidence we get from experience; every time we look at intersecting straight lines, this is further confirmed.

Mill argues that the huge amount of evidence for such propositions makes us think that they have some sort of necessity—some radically different status from other empirically confirmed generalizations. But the only difference is that they are confirmed by a larger number of experiences. The apparent inconceivability of the negation of the axioms of geometry can be explained, Mill claims, psychologically: when a proposition is confirmed so strongly, we become unable to imagine its falsity.

Mill had a similar account of our knowledge of arithmetic. Our knowledge that 5 x 2 = 10, for example, comes inductively from our large number of experiences in which one counts the total number of objects in a group made up of five pairs of them.

Ayer on Mill

You might expect Ayer to endorse Mill's theory. It is just the sort of thing he likes: a radical empiricist view, which is sure to strike traditionalists of all sorts as bizarre. But Ayer rejects it, insisting that the truths of arithmetic and geometry are not justified by induction from experience.

Ayer argues that the question whether some bit of knowledge is a priori or a posteriori is not a question about our cognitive history. He admits that arithmetic is learned in the same way any matters of fact are, and that sense experience is necessary for understanding arithmetical concepts. What he takes to be the crucial point here is that arithmetic does not owe its validity to empirical confirmation.[3] If, for example, '5 x 2 = 10' were known a posteriori, then we could imagine experience that would falsify it. But we cannot.

Suppose, Ayer argues, that you counted the total of what you took to be five pairs of objects, and it came out to be nine. Then you would think that you were wrong to think that there were five pairs to start out with, or that someone had removed one of the objects before you started counting, or that two of them had coalesced, or that you had miscounted. You would not conclude that there was any evidence that 5 times 2 was not 10. So this truth of arithmetic is not confutable by experience. Experiential evidence is irrelevant to its falsification or verification. So it is not a posteriori.

---

[3] *LTL* 74-5.

Ayer offers a similar argument regarding geometry:

> If what appears to be a Euclidean triangle is found by meas-
> urement not to have angles totaling 180 degrees, we do not say
> that we have met with an instance which invalidates the
> mathematical proposition that the sum of the three angles of a
> Euclidean triangle is 180 degrees. We say that we have meas-
> ured wrongly, or, more probably, that the triangle we have
> been measuring is not Euclidean.[4]

Ayer, by the way, goes on to apply the same sort of argument in favor
of his view that the principles of formal logic (his example is the law of
excluded middle) are necessarily true, that no experience would induce
us to reject them. (He unfortunately attributed the view to Mill that
logical truths, like arithmetical and geometrical ones, were a posteriori.
Mill in fact shared Ayer's view, more or less, on logic.)

But Ayer's arguments would not be very persuasive to Mill, who
would freely admit that we would now be strongly, perhaps permanently, disinclined to accept the existence of any evidence against what
we took to be the elementary truths of arithmetic and geometry, and
that we would take the existence of counter-instances to be inconceiv-
able. But inconceivability is psychological, Mill insisted, and it is not
the same thing as impossibility. Ayer, of course, recognizes that what
we are psychologically able or unable to do is not to the point. He is
aware that his argument against Mill about arithmetic is not as conclusive as one would wish:

> In rejecting Mill's theory, we are obliged to be somewhat
> dogmatic. We can do no more than state the issue clearly and
> then trust that his contention will be seen to be discrepant with
> the relevant logical facts.[5]

Ayer's Account of Logic and Mathematics

Ayer's positive account of the justification of arithmetical and
geometrical truths (and of logical ones as well) occurs on the first page
of the Preface to the First Edition of *LTL*. Ayer says:

> I maintain that the reason these [a priori propositions of logic
> and pure mathematics] cannot be confuted in experience is
> that they do not make any assertion about the empirical world,

---

[4] *LTL* 76.
[5] *LTL* 75.

but simply record our determination to use symbols in a certain fashion.[6]

This statement resulted in a great deal of criticism. Here is a typical philosophical reaction to what Ayer appears to be claiming here.

> The linguistic thesis—that necessary propositions are verbal propositions—now seems so obviously false as to be ludicrously so, for it is tantamount to the thesis that necessary propositions are empirical propositions about the use of words.[7]

It appears that he is saying that these propositions are assertions *about* the use of certain bits of language; thus the proposition

A: $2 + 1 = 3$.

would perhaps be equivalent to something like

L: People use the symbols '1', '2', '3' and '+' in a way that makes '2 + 1' synonymous with '3.'

L expresses a fact about the behavior of people who use the language of arithmetic, or perhaps about that language itself, and is clearly synthetic, contingent, and a posteriori.

It would not be surprising to find Ayer claiming that the propositions of arithmetic state contingent facts about the way symbols are used. We have seen him, so far, assuming that the content of a proposition is exhausted by its truth conditions—that is, by the (empirical) facts in the world that obtain if and only if it is true. And, it might seem reasonable to say, the facts in the world that obtain if and only if propositions of arithmetic are true are linguistic facts, facts about the "languages" in which arithmetic symbols occur.

But this is not Ayer's position. To correct this misinterpretation, he writes in the Preface to the Second Edition:

> It has, indeed, been suggested that my treatment of *a priori* propositions makes them into a sub-class of empirical propositions.... That is not, however, the position that I wish to hold; nor do I think that I am committed to it. For although I say that the validity of *a priori* propositions depends upon

---

[6] *LTL* 31.

[7] D. W. Hamlin, "Contingent and Necessary Statements," *The Encyclopedia of Philosophy*, v. 2, 200. Hamlin does not explicitly attribute this view to Ayer, though it appears he has Ayer in mind, and it is easy to see why one might think Ayer held it, on the basis of this quote.

certain facts about verbal usage, I do not think that this is equivalent to saying that they describe these facts in the sense in which empirical propositions may describe the facts that verify them; and indeed I argue that they do not, in this sense, describe any facts at all.[8]

Ayer's claim, then, is that mathematical and logical truths are analytic, depending for their truth solely on the meanings of the language in which they are expressed, but these are not statements *describing* these meaning-facts.

All sentences, of course, depend on the facts of meaning for their truth or falsity. For example, the truth of the sentence 'Pigs don't fly' is partially a consequence of the fact that the constitutive words have the meaning they do. If 'pigs' meant *bats,* then this sentence would be false. But the truth of this sentence in addition depends on the facts about pigs. Analytic truths depend solely on the meanings of the constituent words. For example:

"Either some ants are parasitic or none are" is an analytic proposition. For one need not resort to observation to discover that there either are or are not ants which are parasitic. If one knows what is the function of the words "either," "or," and "not," then one can see that any proposition of the form "Either *p* is true or *p* is not true" is valid, independently of experience. Accordingly, all such propositions are analytic.[9]

Analyticity, as we have seen, provides a good explanation of a priority and of necessity. One need not justify any analytic sentence by empirical observation, because its words alone justify its truth, a priori. They also guarantee its truth, making it impossible that a counterinstance arise, thereby conferring on it (de dicto) necessity.

But are the truths of arithmetic and geometry really analytic? The answer to this question would be forthcoming if we had an adequate account of what analyticity is; as we shall see shortly, an important attack on Ayer's position denies that we can get any such account.

Kant on Analyticity

The distinction between analytic and synthetic judgments was introduced by Kant in his *Critique of Pure Reason.* According to him, an analytic judgment is one in which "the predicate **B** belongs to the sub-

---

[8] *LTL* 17.
[9] *LTL* 79.

ject **A**, as something which is (covertly) contained in this concept **A**." In a synthetic judgment, "**B** lies outside the concept **A**, although it does indeed stand in connection with it." Thus, for example, the judgment that snow is white synthesizes two different concepts, of being snow and of being white; whereas the judgment that bachelors are unmarried merely elucidates the concept of being an bachelor—analyzes it, and extracts its component, being unmarried. The concept of the predicate, 'unmarried,' is "contained in" the concept of the subject, 'bachelors.' Accordingly, for Kant, the predicates of analytic judgments add nothing to the concept of the subject, "merely breaking it up into those constituent concepts that have all along been thought in it."[10]

Ayer does not think that Kant's account of the distinction succeeds in making it clear. He finds the notion of a concept vague, and Kant's presupposition that every judgment is in subject-predicate form, unwarranted. But his main objection is that Kant usually makes this distinction in psychological terms: an analytic judgment is one such that, when someone thinks it, the subjective meaning of the predicate-part of that judgment is contained within the subjective meaning of the subject-part. Ayer says that what Kant needs for the rest of his argument, and what Ayer prefers, is a logical, not a psychological criterion.

Ayer on Analyticity

LTL gives several distinct accounts of analyticity. At one point or another, Ayer defines 'analytic proposition' as:

1. a proposition whose validity depends solely on the definitions of the symbols it contains
2. a proposition whose denial is a self-contradiction
3. a tautology
4. a proposition one can know independently of experience

There are several problems here.

First, we should note that **4** clearly cannot define what Ayer has in mind. The distinction between what can and what cannot be known independently of experience is a different distinction, the epistemological distinction between the a priori and the a posteriori. It should be an open question, not one trivially solved by definition, whether all (or only) analytic truths can be known independently of experience.

There are several problems with **2** and **3**. What Ayer apparently has in mind here is *logical truth*; but his terminology is imprecise, since

---

[10] *Immanuel Kant's Critique of Pure Reason*, tr. Norman Kemp Smith (London: Macmillan and Co., 1934) 30.

43

being a logical truth is not precisely the same thing as being a "tautology" (in the normal way this term is used), nor is the denial of every logical truth a self-contradiction (which is, strictly speaking, a conjunction of the affirmation and the denial of some statement).

But there are more important problems here. One is that if Ayer defines 'analytic' as *logically true*, this begs the question of the analyticity of logical truths; it makes this claim trivial, definitional. This claim would not, then, give us any insight into the source of our knowledge of logical truths. Another is that Ayer wants to include statements like 'All oculists are eye-doctors' among the analytic truths, and this is not, strictly speaking, a *logical* truth.

Let us then turn to 1: An analytic proposition is a proposition whose validity (Ayer appears merely to mean *truth* by "validity") depends solely on the definitions of the symbols it contains.

This appears broad enough to encompass all the examples Ayer intends, and it does not beg any questions. It seems plausible that propositions like 'All oculists are eye-doctors' is true merely because of the definitions of the symbols it contains (though we shall later question this); Ayer will have to make a case, however, for the much less plausible claim that propositions of mathematics, geometry, and logic are of this sort. All this soon.

Propositions? Sentences? Statements?

You may have noticed that in our discussion so far we have sometimes been calling the things that are analytic or synthetic, "propositions." Ayer normally calls them this, though he sometimes also calls them "sentences," "utterances," or "statements." These are by no means the same sort of thing. He also uses these terms more or less interchangeably in referring to the things that are analytic (or synthetic), the things that are believed on the basis of experience, the things capable of empirical verification, and so on.

Ayer became aware that there was a problem in his way of speaking, and attempted to fix it in his Introduction to the Second Edition. The first problem Ayer saw was that his distinction between meaningful (because verifiable) and meaningless (because unverifiable) "*propositions*" would not do. *Sentences* come in meaningful and meaningless varieties, but *propositions*, which (on one view) are what sentences express, are the meanings of meaningful sentences, so there are no propositions associated with meaningless sentences, and no meaningless propositions. In the First Edition, he tried to avoid this difficulty by speaking of "putative propositions"—presumably what meaningless sentences would express but do not—or of the propositions which meaningless sentences "purport" to express. But for several reasons, by the time he prepared the second edition, Ayer found this unsatisfactory; the main reason is that he came to prefer to say that meaningless sentences expressed nothing.

He considers, then, saying instead that *sentences* are what are verifiable or unverifiable. But he is unhappy with this as well, because it seems clear to him that it is not exactly particular sentences that are verified; for there is no difference between verifying "The cat is on the mat" and "The mat is what the cat is on" and "The mat is under the cat" and "The feline is on the mat" and "*Le chat se trouve sur le petit tapis.*" These are different sentences, but it is what they all equally express that is verified by the appropriate observations.

His response is to introduce a technical term, 'statement.' Any form of words that is "grammatically significant" makes a statement, even ones like 'God loves me' which (he thinks) is meaningless and expresses no proposition. Any two intertranslatable sentences make the same statement. Statements are what are verified; the lack of verification conditions for a statement is what makes it (or any sentence expressing it) meaningless.

Ayer leaves the matter here, though as you might suspect, philosophers would want to know a whole lot more about what a statement is supposed to be, exactly, and what its connection is with meanings.

But now let us turn to a closely related difficulty that Ayer does not deal with explicitly. We have been considering his claim that "analytic propositions" are true solely because of the definitions of the symbols or words involved, but we can see now that this cannot be right. Propositions do not have symbols or words in them: only sentences do. But on the other hand, Ayer might not want to say that sentences are the things that are true or false because of these definitions, because it is not sentences that are true or false: it is what one says by means of these sentences, or the content of what one thinks and expresses by them. It is at least something like the meaning of the words involved, not the words themselves, that (without assistance) makes analytic items true. Two different intertranslatable analytic sentences are analytic for the same reason, despite the fact that they are composed of different words. Perhaps Ayer's "statements," rather than propositions or sentences, will be the appropriate objects to count as analytic or synthetic; but we should have to figure out a lot more about what statements are, and to answer many questions Ayer did not deal with, before we knew if this suggestion has any plausibility.

Quine on the Analytic/Synthetic Distinction

The most influential criticism of Ayer's version of the analytic/synthetic distinction was published by Willard Quine in his 1951 article "Two Dogmas of Empiricism."[11] Quine notes that to make this distinction, one would need a good account of synonymy. Ayer says that

O: All oculists are eye-doctors.

is analytic, because its truth follows from the meaning of the symbols 'oculists' and 'eye-doctors' alone, because 'oculists' and 'eye-doctors' are synonymous. But (Quine's example)

C: All creatures with a heart are creatures with kidneys.

would be, in Ayer's judgment, synthetic, because 'creatures with a heart' is not synonymous with 'creatures with kidneys.'

'Oculists' and 'eye-doctors' are co-extensive terms (i.e., they refer to the same set of things, but so are 'creatures with a heart' and 'creatures with kidneys.' The fact that each is a co-extensive pair has the consequence that both **O** and **C** are true. So what is the difference?

Quine argues that attempts to explain this supposed difference must go in a circle. For example, one might say that the **O** is a necessary truth, while **C** is merely contingent; but, of course, if one gave (as Ayer does) an account of necessity which reduces it to analyticity, then we are back where we started. Or one might say, as Ayer does, that the difference here is that the truth of **O** is the result of the existence of a semantical (i.e., *meaning*) rule of language relating 'oculists' and 'eye-doctors,' but there is no corresponding semantical rule relating 'creatures with a heart' and 'creatures with kidneys.' But Quine argues that this approach similarly goes nowhere. How do we distinguish between something that is a semantical rule (which presumably would instruct us to interchange the terms 'oculists' and 'eye-doctors' in sentences whenever we liked) from something that is a biological fact (which would allow interchange of the terms 'animals with hearts' and 'animals with kidneys')?

---

[11] The original version of this was published in the *Philosophical Review*, 1951; 60, 20-43. A slightly amended version, from which page citations will be made here, is in Quine, *From a Logical Point of View*, (Cambridge: Harvard University Press, 1953; revised ed. 1961).

Quine concludes:

> For all its a priori reasonableness, a boundary between ana-
> lytic and synthetic statements has not been drawn. That there
> is such a distinction to be drawn at all is an unempirical
> dogma of empiricists, a metaphysical article of faith.[12]

Quine's objection, that one cannot give a good non-circular account of this difference, did not serve to convince everyone that there is
no difference.[13] The distinction, after all, does have, as Quine admits,
"a priori reasonableness."

Are All A Priori Statements Analytic?

We shall put these difficulties aside now, and turn to consideration
of Ayer's claims that arithmetic, geometry, and logical truths are analytic and a priori.

Arguing that geometry is analytic, Ayer says:

> The axioms of a geometry are simply definitions, and… the
> theorems of a geometry are simply the logical consequences of
> these definitions.[14]

One might doubt that definitions and their logical consequences
could tell you anything substantial about the world; and Ayer is in en-
tire sympathy:

> A geometry is not in itself about physical space; in itself it
> cannot be said to be "about" anything. But we can use a ge-
> ometry to reason about physical space. That is to say, once we
> have given the axioms a physical interpretation, we can pro-
> ceed to apply the theorems to the objects which satisfy the
> axioms. Whether a geometry can be applied to the actual
> physical world or not, is an empirical question which falls out-
> side the scope of geometry itself…. All that the geometry it-
> self tells us is that if anything can be brought under the defini-
> tions, it will also satisfy the theorems. It is therefore a purely
> logical system, and its propositions are purely analytic propo-
> sitions.[15]

---

[12] Quine 37.

[13] The best-known defense of the analytic/synthetic distinction in reply
to Quine's objections is "In Defence of a Dogma," by H. P. Grice and
P. F. Strawson, *Philosophical Review* 65 (1956) 141-158.

[14] *LTL* 82.

[15] *LTL* 82-3.

So, for example, we might give the term 'straight line' in geometry the physical interpretation of the path of a ray of light; then we can ask the empirical question whether triangles in space (whose sides were the paths of light-rays) had interior angles adding up to exactly 180°. The answer turns out to be no. But this does not show, according to Ayer, that Euclidean geometry contains a false statement about triangles; what it shows is that this is not a proper physical interpretation for 'straight line.'

Similarly, Ayer argues that arithmetic is analytic:

> Our knowledge that no observation can ever confute the proposition "7 + 5 = 12: depends simply on the fact that the symbolic expression "7 + 5" is synonymous with "12."[16]

and this seems rather less plausible than the other claims. Kant argues:

> We might, indeed, at first suppose that the proposition 7 + 5 = 12 is a merely analytic proposition.... But if we look more closely we find that the concept of the sum of 7 and 5 contains nothing save the union of the two numbers into one, and in this no thought is being taken as to what that single number may be which combines both. The concept of 12 is by no means already thought in merely thinking this union of 7 and 5; and I may analyze my concept of such a possible sum as long as I please, still I shall never find the 12 in it.[17]

Ayer replies that Kant is mistakenly applying a psychological criterion for analyticity here: psychologically, one might well think of the sum of seven and five without thinking of twelve; but this is not relevant to the question whether that statement is analytic. (Ayer unfortunately continues by claiming that what does show that it is analytic is that it cannot be denied without self-contradiction;[18] but, as we have seen, this will not do either.)

Ayer's view about arithmetic parallels his view about geometry: since every truth in arithmetic is merely true by definition, nothing is being said about the world. To get truths about the world, we would have to provide a way of interpreting the abstract terms in arithmetic to apply to real objects. Suppose, then, that we provide this interpretation, and arithmetic thus physically interpreted predicted that if you measured out seven liters of a liquid in one container, and five liters of a

---

[16] *LTL* 85.
[17] Kant 33.
[18] *LTL* 78.

liquid in another container, and poured both into one big container, then that big container would contain twelve liters. But experiment shows that mixing seven liters of alcohol with five liters of water results in somewhat less than twelve liters of liquid. Ayer would say that this does not show that $7 + 5 = 12$ is not always true. What it shows is that this interpretation of the symbols of arithmetic—this application to the real world—is improper. It does not count as an instance of '$7 + 5$.'

Ayer's point here is really quite simple. If a language gives a definition to a term, and if certain statements follow from that definition, then these truths are a priori and necessary. The reason they are necessary is that something in the real world could not count as fitting that definition unless it fit those statements. So, for example, the reason why any bachelor must be unmarried is that we do not allow it to count as a bachelor unless it is unmarried; this is a consequence of the definition of the word 'bachelor.' Similarly, Ayer argues, we do not allow anything to count as an instance of $7 + 5$ unless it also is 12. This is Ayer's account of all a priori and all necessary statements.

In general, there are two sorts of reactions we might have when we encounter what might be taken to be a counter-instance of a well-entrenched belief. We might take it to be a genuine counter-instance, and decide that, after all and despite conventional wisdom and previous experience, it has turned out that that well-entrenched belief was false. On the other hand, we might take it that, despite appearances, this new instance did not count as a counter-instance, because it was not what that well-entrenched belief was about. Quine agrees that there is a difference here: sometimes we react one way and sometimes the other. But he argues that this difference does not reflect any supposed distinction between what is true by definition and what is on the other hand a well-established empirical generalization. This difference is rather a consequence of considerations of conservative cognitive economy; roughly speaking, we adjust things in response to a cognitive anomaly in the way that will necessitate the smallest shakeup in our interconnected "web of belief." If Quine is right, then, there is no real distinction between a truth-by-definition and an empirically well-established matter of fact. The only real distinction is between beliefs that are strongly entrenched and difficult to give up given putative counter-examples, and those that would more easily be abandoned.

Consider, for example, the strongly entrenched belief that maple trees shed their leaves in the fall. Imagine that a tree in the back-yard of the house you have recently moved into looks for all the world just like a maple tree, but it turns out not to shed its leaves in the fall. You might very well conclude that, despite appearances, that was not a maple tree at all. But this is not a matter of your taking leaf-shedding to be part of the definition of 'maple tree.' You have the choice of rejecting the belief that all maples shed their leaves in the fall, or of rejecting the belief that the tree in question is a maple, and you choose to reject the latter.

The only distinction worth making here, Quine would say, is the distinction between well-entrenched beliefs and the rest: the latter are more easily amended, given apparently recalcitrant experience, than the former. So Quine allows something like a relative a priori/a posteriori distinction (now a matter of how empirically revisable a belief is), but denies that this is accounted for by any account relying on the distinction, which he argues is spurious, between truth-by-definition and matter-of-fact.

Necessity

We have been concentrating on Ayer's use of the analytic/-synthetic distinction to give an account of the difference between a priori and a posteriori knowledge. He also deployed it to explain the difference between necessary and contingent facts—a metaphysical, not an epistemological matter. Ayer's account of necessity is that it simply is analyticity. Because these necessary-because-analytic propositions are, in a way, empty—merely trivial definitional truths, not full-blooded facts at all—Ayer's position is more like a denial of the existence of necessity than an account of it.

Quine, of course, having argued against the analytic/synthetic distinction, could not give even Ayer's thin linguistic account of necessity. Quine's position is that the only real distinction here is between those statements that we are relatively more/less willing to abandon under the pressure of recalcitrant experience, and that this would do as well to account for what philosophers thought was a metaphysical difference between the necessary and the contingent. Ayer and Quine agree, then, in refusing necessity the full status it has commonly been accorded in philosophy.

But Saul Kripke's publication in 1974 of *Naming and Necessity*[19] did a great deal to rehabilitate full-fledged metaphysical necessity. Kripke relies on the traditional account of necessity as truth in all possible worlds. In this way of understanding necessity, to say that something is not necessary, merely contingent, is to say that it is false in

---

[19] Most widely available now in book form (Cambridge: Harvard University Press, 1980).

some possible worlds. Thus, the contingency of the proposition *Aristotle is wise* means that there are some possible worlds in which Aristotle is not wise. But, Kripke points out, when we consider the set of possible worlds and say that Aristotle is wise in some of them and not wise in others, we are designating the same thing—which we call Aristotle—in all those worlds. In some of the worlds in which he exists, he is wise, and in some not, but in all of those worlds he is Aristotle. (It is not necessary that he was *named* Aristotle—a contingent matter; what is necessary is that he is *that person* Aristotle.) So proper names designate the same thing in each possible world, and *being Aristotle* is a property that this thing has necessarily—in every possible world in which it exists. Thus, though your height is contingent (there are some possible worlds in which you are taller than you are in this, actual, world), there are no worlds in which you are a different person. Similarly, Kripkeans argue, it is contingent that water is colorless, but necessary that it is H_2O.[20]

The Kripke view of necessity has remained controversial, but the philosophical community has become much more willing to consider genuine necessity. Ayer, however, remained unrepentant on this matter, speaking of Kripkeism as a "relapse into the quagmire of metaphysical necessity."[21] In conversation about Kripke, Ayer called his arguments "perverse," "disingenuous" and "absurd" and said, "Earlier in this century a few of us moved philosophy on a notch or two. I am not going to live to see it put back."[22]

---

[20] See, for example, Hilary Putnam, *Mind, Language and Reality. Philosophical Papers, Volume 2* (Cambridge: Cambridge UP, 1975).
[21] "Reply to Hilary Putnam," in Hahn.
[22] Rogers 311.

5
Other Minds and
Other Matters

Problems with the Verification Criterion

Reactions to the First Edition of *LTL* from the philosophical community were highly polarized; Ayer's verification criterion drew the strongest criticisms at its points of application. In this and the next chapter, we shall take a look at several areas where Ayer's application of his principles had what many philosophers considered wildly implausible results, and at Ayer's reactions to their criticisms.

The Past

Ayer faces this dilemma: either statements about the past are meaningless, because unverifiable, or else they can be verified by present and future experiences, in which case they would really be disguised statements about the present or the future.

Suppose, for example, that you set the timer on your automatic coffee maker to turn on at 6 am, while you are still asleep, so that there will be fresh coffee when you wake up at 7 am. Now, the next morning, you find hot coffee in the machine, confirming this statement:

P: The coffee maker made coffee early this morning.

Your present experiences—seeing the coffee, smelling it, and so on—verify **P** for you now, in the morning; but these are experiences of present events and objects. If these give the meaning of **P**, then **P** must actually be about present events and objects, not past ones as it appears.

So if the cognitive meaning—the factual content—of a statement for a person at a time is given by the experiences that would verify or falsify that statement for that person, then statements "about the past" turn out actually to be concerned with the present or the future, not with the past at all. **P** of course, appears to be about an event that happened in the recent past, at 6 am, but when we examine its verification conditions, we find that it cannot literally be about a past event. Ayer says:

> I do not find anything excessively paradoxical in the view that propositions about the past are rules for the prediction of those "historical" experiences which are commonly said to verify them, and I do not see how else "our knowledge of the past" is to be analysed.[1]

But, of course, many other philosophers have found this view "excessively paradoxical."

Ayer defends his view by considering what might be the alternative. He suspects, he says, that those who object to his view are doing so on the basis of the assumption that the past

> is somehow 'objectively there' to be corresponded to—that it is "real" in the metaphysical sense of the term. And…it is clear that such an assumption is not a genuine hypothesis.[2]

The Past: Second Edition

But by the time he was preparing the Second Edition, he appears to have come to the view that this position might be excessively paradoxical after all. He says this in the Introduction to the Second Edition:

> By saying of propositions about the past that they are "rules for the prediction of those 'historical' experiences which are commonly said to verify them" I seem to imply that they can somehow be translated into propositions about present or future experiences. But this is certainly incorrect. Statements about the past may be verifiable in the sense that when they are conjoined with other premises of a suitable kind they may entail observation statements which do not follow from these other premises alone; but I do not think that the truth of any observation-statements which refer to the present or the future is a necessary condition of the truth of any statement about the past.[3]

We noted in Chapter 3 that at some point after he published the First Edition of *LTL* Ayer changed his mind about the possibility of a

---

[1] *LTL* 102.
[2] *LTL* 102.
[3] *LTL* 18-19.

simple phenomenalist account of statements of fact, amending his view to take account of the fact that the experiences associated with a factual statement would be expected to occur only under certain circumstances. The way Ayer puts this is that the factual statements entail the experience statements only when they are conjoined with "other premises of a suitable kind"—i.e., those asserting the obtaining of the conditions under which the experiences would be expected.

Thus statement **P** would entail that there are certain experiences there to be had under certain circumstances; so **P** conjoined with suitable other factual assumptions (that my eyes are open, pointed in the right direction, and functioning properly, that nobody has removed all the coffee from the machine after 6 am, and so on) entails the existence of the appropriate present verifying visual coffee experiences. And there are other present or future experiences I could have which would equally be entailed by that statement, given other appropriate factual assumptions about the surrounding conditions.

But this does not solve Ayer's problem. Recall his distinction between experiences that count merely as evidence for a proposition, and those that are supposed to count as constituting the meaning of that proposition. The observations we make now or in the future to confirm **P** must be of the first sort—otherwise Ayer would have to conclude implausibly that **P** was about the present or the future. But there are no other confirming experiences (now) available. So it appears that there are none that constitute the meaning of **P**. Must **P** then be meaningless?

Verifiability in Principle (Again)

But all this might seem to be entirely the wrong way for a verificationist to deal with the meaning of statements about the past. If there is any hope of understanding the meaning of **P** in terms of experiences that would verify it, it must be that these experiences must be of the event spoken of in **P**—must be, that is, experiences of what happened at 6 am. Of course, you were asleep when that event happened, and nobody else was there; and now, at 7 am, it is impossible for you to witness that past event. So nobody had any of the experiences of the event itself, and now it is impossible that anyone get them; but it is nevertheless the case that *had* anyone been there, that person would have had certain experiences.

In the Introduction to the Second Edition, Ayer remarks that the trouble with statements about the past, that they are translatable into hypothetical observations which the observer is incapable of, is not a special peculiarity of these statements;

for it is true also of unfulfilled conditionals about the present that their protases[4] cannot in fact be satisfied, since they require of the observer that he should be occupying a different spatial position from that which he actually does.[5]

As we have noted, what he requires for these observation-statements is not observation in fact, but merely observability in principle: the observations do not have to be ones we are actually capable of carrying out. In his example of assertions about the far side of the moon, we say merely that if we were in a spatial location that we are currently unable to assume, then we would have such-and-such an experience. Similarly here, in the case of assertions about the past, we say that if we were in a temporal location that happens now to be unavailable to us, then we would have this-and-that experience.

Critics have complained that Ayer's notion of observability is not as clear as it might be. There is an obvious difference between the "observability" of current events elsewhere and past events. It seems that I am now capable of observing current events elsewhere because I am now capable of making true their conditions for observation—by going to where they are happening. But I am not now capable of going to the past, where past events happened. Time-travel, it seems, may be more than merely practically impossible.

Ayer does not want the distinction between what one is capable of in principle but not in fact, and what one is genuinely incapable of, to be based on the observer's contingent psychological or physical abilities. Sometimes he says that a proposition would be nonsense if there were no "conceivable" observations that would confirm it. But conceivability again appears to be a psychological test. He says that he wants the distinction to be a "logical" one: something is observable in principle when its observation is *logically* (rather than physically or psychologically) possible. But this is not helpful, and may be overstating things. A paradigm example of a meaningless statement for Ayer would be the mystic's assertion, "Reality is one"; but would we really want to say that it is *logically* impossible for someone to observe that this is the case? Remembering that Ayer uses the term 'logically impossible' in a wide sense equivalent to *analytically false*, would we say that it is analytically false to affirm that someone observed that reality is one?

---

[4] The protasis is the antecedent of a conditional statement, the part that occurs between the 'if' and the 'then.'

[5] *LTL* 19.

The distinction we have been worrying about is a difficult one to give a rigorous account of, but it does appear to have some degree of plausibility. Understanding the meaning of a factual statement is understanding what observations one would have under certain conditions— whether or not it is in any practical sense possible (or "conceivable") that one might get into those conditions. Statements about events in the past, then, do have a clear meaning when they entail observations one would have had were one witnessing those events. Ayer is right that this has nothing to do with verification *in practice*, and that this is not a special problem for statements about the past. Even the presence of the cat in the next room right now is, in a way, unobservable by me in practice, because by the time I opened the door and walked in there to take a look, this instantaneous event will be past and gone.

Other Minds

One cannot observe the mental states of others. Some philosophers have argued that we nevertheless can infer their existence by analogy with one's own case. I laugh when I find things funny, and although I cannot directly detect the mental event of your finding something funny, I can assume that your laughing shows that you find something funny.

But Ayer argues that this "argument from analogy" is worthless: "No argument can render probable a completely unverifiable hypothesis."[6] If others' mental states could never conceivably be manifested in my experience, the assertion that they exist is "metaphysical" and "senseless." So if other people are identified as other minds, the assertion that other people exist is equally nonsense.

But this conclusion is absurd. Where has it gone wrong?

The mistake Ayer diagnoses here is the identification of other people with their minds—as constructions out of inaccessibly hidden mental events. Clearly, he says, the assumption that other people's experiences are completely inaccessible to my observation is false. We *can* observe "mental" facts about others. He gives examples: I can observe that two people have the same color sense, for example, by seeing that they sort colored things out in the same way. I can observe that someone understands me by seeing that my utterances have the effect on that person's actions that I regard as appropriate. When I see you laughing, I see that you find something funny.

---

[6] *LTL* 129.

It is important to see here that Ayer is not arguing that your laughter is evidence for me, even very good evidence, for your finding something funny. Your laughter would be good evidence for this if it were regularly associated with it. Ayer's view here is that what I am seeing here is *the fact itself.* Your laughter is not evidence that you find something funny—it *constitutes* your finding something funny—at least, as far as I am concerned.

Ayer's position here is a variety of philosophical behaviorism, a position that attracted many philosophers and psychologists between about 1925 and the late fifties, but whose day is past. The fact that the heyday of behaviorism was roughly simultaneous with that of Logical Positivism is no accident: verificationist principles led philosophers and psychologists to behaviorism. A central and fatal argument against philosophical behaviorism was a special case of the general argument we have been looking at against phenomenalism, that one simply cannot provide a list of actual or potential experiences which give the meaning of factual statements—in this case, statements attributing mental states to others.

But even those who favored a behaviorist analysis of attributions of mental states to others felt uncomfortable in applying it to self-attributions. I verify that you find something funny by hearing you laugh, but I surely do not verify that I find something funny by hearing myself laugh. Ayer agrees, but this leads him to a position with possibly even greater implausibility: that it means something different when I say that I find something funny and when I say that you do. My assertions about my own mental states get their meaning from their verification by my introspection of my own private mental contents, so they signify these inner states when I talk about myself. But my assertions about your mental states get their meaning from their verification by my observing your behavior, so they signify your outer behavior. Thus, implausibly, when I say that I find something funny, I am referring to an entirely different sort of thing than when I say that you do.

Second Thoughts about Other Minds

Four years after the first edition of *LTL* appeared, Ayer published *The Foundations of Empirical Knowledge.* It is clear that the implausibility of his LTL position on other minds had been worrying him, and in his *FEK* he argued for a considerably different position. There he attempted to apply roughly the same strategy to the other minds problem as he used in the problem of statements about the past—that direct verification, of the kind which gives the meaning of attributions, is possible—but only in principle, not in fact.

In *FEK*, Ayer worries at length over whether it is really impossible that one have another's experiences.[7] In one sense, it seems, it really is impossible—really logically impossible, not merely practically impossible. For whatever I imagine experiencing is *my* experience. But on the other hand, perhaps I can imagine experiencing someone else's experiences. Suppose that my own recent experiential history consists of experiences **A**, **B**, and **C**, and yours of experiences **D**, **E**, and **F**. Now imagine that instead of **F**'s having happened to you, it happened to me; then my history would have been (say) of experiences **A**, **B**, **F**. Would I not then have had an experience that was (in fact) yours? If it is a contingent matter that my history of experiences consists in one string rather than another, sense can be made of the counterfactual supposition that I had a different set of experiences, including one that was in fact yours. What I am doing here, in effect, is imagining myself in your place.

This is clearly verification in principle only. But because this verifiability in principle gives sense to attributions of private mental states to others, we can confirm the existence of these private states *indirectly*—not by experiencing them, but by experiencing other things which are good evidence for them. I know in my own case that various behaviors are reliably correlated with particular mental states, so I can take similar behaviors to be evidence for like mental states in you. The argument from the analogy of one's own case is rehabilitated.

The problem of making sense of statements attributing mental states to others is one that continued to bother Ayer. A few years after publishing *FEK*, he wrote this in the Introduction to the Second Edition of *LTL*:

> I confess that I am doubtful whether the account that is given
> in this book is correct; but I am not convinced that it is not. In
> [*FEK*] I argued that…there is a sense in which "it is not logi-
> cally inconceivable that I should have an experience that is in
> fact owned by someone else"…. More recently, however, I
> have come to think that this reasoning is very dubious. For
> while it is possible to imagine circumstances in which we
> might have found it convenient to say of two different persons
> that they owned the same experience, the fact is that, accord-
> ing to our present usage, it is a necessary proposition that they

---

[7] *FEK* Chapter III, "The Egocentric Predicament."

do not.... Consequently, I am inclined to revert to a "behav-iouristic" interpretation of propositions about other people's experiences. But I own that it has an air of paradox which prevents me from being wholly confident that it is true.[8]

In *The Problem of Knowledge* (1956), he criticized a behavioristic reduction of mentalistic ascriptions to others as an example of the sort of *LTL* reductionism he was by then renouncing, on the grounds that it mistakenly took evidence for something to be the thing itself.[9]

Theoretical Entities

Science was important to the members of the Vienna Circle. They shared the idea that the empirical methods of science represented the paradigm of good epistemological practice, especially by comparison with the a priori speculative philosophical methodology for which they had such disdain. It was therefore a matter of concern that the basic principles developed by the Circle appeared to attack the legitimacy of an important conceptual element of science, the theoretical entity. This is an object which is postulated by scientific theories, but which is entirely unobservable, even in principle. Examples of theoretical entities are the electron and the magnetic field. The problem with observing an electron is not merely that it is too small. It is rather that, given the physics of the electron and of observation, nothing could even count as observing one. All we can observe, it seems, is its effects.

It is clear why such entities are problematic for radically empiricist philosophers, and also how they might respond: by insisting that statements about these things are really about the experiences by which one detects them.

But this reductionism is quite implausible. Consider, for example, the attempt to define 'temperature' in terms of various conditional observations. One way we observe temperature is by looking at the length of the column on a mercury thermometer; another way is by observing the electrical resistance on a platinum-wire thermometer. But it seems that none of these experiences is experience of temperature *itself*—each of them is only an experience of its effects.

Ayer on Theoretical Entities

The problem of theoretical entities is in a way like the other two problems we have looked at in this chapter. In all three cases, we can-

---

[8] *LTL* 19-20.
[9] *PK* 79-80.

not have experiences that would verify the existence of the entity—all we can experience is its effects. As we have seen, Ayer (at times) attempted to deal with the past and with other minds by claiming that one's inability to experience the entities in question here was only a practical matter, and that the assertions in question really were associated with verifying experiences which we happen to be in the wrong position to have. But this will not work for theoretical entities, because there is *no* position in which one would have a directly verifying experience of the presence of such things. Nothing could even count as experiencing them. They are unverifiable in principle.

In the Introduction to the Second Edition of *LTL*, Ayer responds to the problem of theoretical entities in this way:

> In giving my account of the conditions in which a statement is to be considered indirectly verifiable, I have explicitly put in the proviso that the "other premises" may include analytic statements; and my reason for doing this is that I intend in this way to allow for the case of scientific theories which are expressed in terms that do not themselves designate anything observable. For while the statements that contain these terms may not appear to describe anything that anyone could ever observe, a "dictionary" may be provided by means of which they can be transformed into statements that are verifiable; and the statements which constitute the dictionary can be regarded as analytic. Were this not so, there would be nothing to choose between such scientific theories and those that I should dismiss as metaphysical.[10]

Consider the example of temperature. Ayer is suggesting that theories of heat provide a "dictionary" which gives meaning to ideas like "rise in temperature" by associating it *definitionally* with observable effects such as the rising column of mercury in a thermometer. So these effects are not merely contingently associated with the entity or phenomenon in question: they are part of its definition. That there are or would be these effects under the appropriate circumstances is all that is meant when the existence of the theoretical item is asserted. In this way, Ayer allows for meaningful talk of certain unobservables.

Compare this with the way he dealt with the objection that 'God exists' is not nonsense, because verifiable by observation of orderly features of the physical world. (This was discussed above, in Chapter 3.) In both cases, we are supposed to be able to observe only effects of

---

[10] *LTL* 13-14.

the object in question, never the object itself. But effects constitute the definition of theoretical entities, but not of 'God.' What we *mean* when we speak of a theoretical entity is: whatever it is that causes or would cause this or that effect under certain conditions. 'God,' by contrast, is associated by definition with no verifying experiences.

Ayer's idea here appears to anticipate the category later philosophers have come to call *functional kinds*: these are defined wholly in terms of their causes and/or effects. 'Can-opener' for example is defined as anything that has the effect of making a closed can into an open one. Of course, we can directly observe a can-opener, and know that one is there by means other than observation of its effects. The point is, however, that the legitimacy of such definitions appears to open the way for Ayer's account of the meaningfulness of names of purely theoretical objects, which also are defined wholly in terms of causes and/or effects.

One would have liked to have seen Ayer apply this sort of move to the problem of other minds. To treat mental attributions as functional would be to understand them as asserting not the existence of certain external behaviors (this is behaviorism), but rather the existence of an internal entity, whatever it might be, that *causes* that external behavior. Functionalism about other minds has become an attractive theory to many philosophers during the past couple of decades.

We have seen Ayer move away from the simple and radical verificationalism in *LTL* to save the meaningfulness of certain kinds of talk. In the next chapter, we shall examine two areas—ethics and religion— in which *LTL* verificationism had results that were implausible to many philosophers, but in which Ayer did not retreat; instead, he argued that talk here really was without cognitive significance.

61

6
Religion and Ethics

The Meaninglessness of Religious Utterances

Ayer produces a brief argument in *LTL* that the existence of God cannot be demonstratively certain, for it is not a tautology nor can it be derived from tautologies. Then he goes on to consider at greater length the possibility that 'God exists' is an empirical proposition. If it were a significant factual claim, he argues, then it would be possible, in the usual way, to deduce verification conditions from it that would express its meaning. But the supposed evidence for God does not constitute what anyone *means* by theological talk. (So God does not have the status of a scientific theoretical entity.)

Ayer's point, then, is even if believers would count certain experiences as evidence for (or against) the existence of God, this does not render assertions that God exists meaningful. And you cannot have evidence for a meaningless assertion.

Ayer may be right that religious utterances do not characteristically have cognitive significance. One bit of evidence for this is the context of religious talk: churches are quite dissimilar to institutions for gathering evidence, for example, scientific laboratories and newspaper offices. Many religious people would be puzzled by the idea that belief in God is similar to ordinary factual belief in mundane facts, needing justification by empirical evidence. A good deal of religious utterance does not even display the surface form of assertion; it is, instead, for example, very often supplication, praise, celebration, chant or song. And when religious talk has assertive form, what is said is often taken to have vanishingly small empirical significance. For example, "God will always provide what you really need" might be more properly taken to be expressive or poetic or ceremonial, rather than informative or cognitive; religious people's actions sometimes appear to show that they do not take it literally.

Notwithstanding all this, there is a significantly widespread view among religious people that a good deal of what religion says has ordinary factual significance. This was amply demonstrated by the great quantity of hostility Ayer's views generated among the religious.

His suggestion in effect that religious utterance be consigned to the garbage heap is directed solely at its pretension to factual truth. As we have seen, he is well aware that language-use is not restricted to fact-stating, and when he claims that the lack of verification-conditions renders an utterance meaningless, he is talking only about *cognitive* meaning, and recognizes that "meaning" in a larger sense refers also to a wide variety of psychological functions of language.

Mysticism

The mystical religious tradition agrees with Ayer that religious language cannot have the same sort of cognitive meaning as everyday or scientific assertions. Mystics sometimes say that talk about God is nevertheless not cognitive nonsense, but rather a necessarily inadequate attempt to utter inexpressible truths. Against the mystic, Ayer argues:

> If [the mystic] allows that it is impossible to define God in in-
> telligible terms, ... then he must also admit that he is bound to
> talk nonsense when he describes it.... It is no use his saying
> that he has apprehended facts but is unable to express them.
> For we know that if he really had acquired any information, he
> would be able to express it. He would be able to indicate in
> some way or other how the genuineness of his discovery
> might be empirically determined. The fact that he cannot re-
> veal what he "knows,"...shows that his state of mystical intui-
> tion is not a genuinely cognitive state. So that in describing his
> vision the mystic does not give us any information about the
> external world.[1]

Wittgenstein's work has found some favor among contemporary philosophers with a mystical religious bent. Ayer read Wittgenstein's *Tractatus* during the late 1920s, and, as we have noted, reports that "it made an overwhelming impression on me." But:

> I disregarded the hint of mysticism which occurs towards the
> end. Wholeheartedly accepting Wittgenstein's dictum *Wovon*

---

[1] *LTL* 118-119.

> *man nicht sprechen kann, darüber muss man schweigen*—
> somewhat archaically rendered on Ogden's translation as
> 'Whereof one cannot speak, therof one must be silent'—I ig-
> nored Wittgenstein's suggestion that what could not be stated
> might nevertheless be shown.[2]

He approvingly quotes F. P. Ramsey on this: "What you can't say, you
can't say and you can't whistle it either."[3] Ayer has nothing against
whistling, of course; he is arguing merely that this is not a way of saying something.

Ayer's treatment of religion is entirely negative, directed against
the claim that it has cognitive significance, and he has very little to say
about what the function of religious talk might then be (if anything).
His position on ethical talk is similar—he thinks ethics also fails to
make factual assertions—but he has a good deal to say about what it
does instead.

Against Ethical Naturalism

'Ethical naturalism' is the name of a family of ethical theories that
share the view that ethical terms are equivalent, by definition, to terms
naming some "natural" property—that is, that they may be defined
wholly in terms of non-evaluative descriptions of the world or of human psychology.

One example of a naturalistic ethical theory is utilitarianism. Varieties of this theory proposes to define 'right action' as an action that
leads, in the long run, to the greatest balance of happiness over unhappiness, or of pleasure over pain, or of satisfied over unsatisfied desire,
in sum, for everyone affected. Another is what Ayer calls "subjectiv-
ism," (often called "egoism" nowadays), which defines 'right action' as
the action which leads to pleasure (or other states) for the speaker.

We might expect Ayer to endorse some form of ethical naturalism.
In identifying right action by definition with some empirically observable state, it would make ethical assertions verifiable and cognitively
meaningful. Historically, empiricists have been attracted to ethical
naturalism. John Stuart Mill, of course, was a utilitarian, and one might
make a case that Hume was one also.

But Ayer cannot accept these theories. What they propose cannot
be correct definitions of 'right action,' Ayer argues, because it is not
"self-contradictory" (i.e., analytically false, false-by-definition) to say

---

[2] *PML* 115.
[3] *PML* 115.

that an action has any one of these characteristics but is nevertheless not the right thing to do. Ayer's argument here is borrowed with little change from G. E. Moore, who presents it this way: consider any "natural" characteristic, **C**, in terms of which it is proposed that 'right action' might be defined. But given that an action has **C**, it is still an open question whether it is right.[4] Compare with this the fact that it is not an open question whether, given the fact that someone is an oculist, that person is an eye-doctor.

This is not really an argument for the position that ethical terms have no naturalistic definition; it is not much more than a restatement of the position. But it is hard to see what would count as a general argument here. Ayer invites us to consider some samples of proposed definitions, hoping that we should see that none of these is correct, and that we should be convinced that ethical terms are not definitionally equivalent with any natural ones.

Ethical Intuitionism

Moore was enough of an empiricist to think that knowledge of the presence or absence of natural characteristics is determined only through one's physical senses. But (he thought) ethical properties are not identical with any natural property—they are "non-natural"—so their presence or absence cannot be detected by the ordinary physical senses. What detects them is a special moral sense—a faculty for moral perception Moore calls "intuition."

For Moore, then, ethical statements are synthetic, but their epistemological status is puzzling. If a posteriori knowledge is what we must use our ordinary sense-organs to get, then ethical knowledge might be considered a priori. (Kant can be interpreted as an ethical intuitionist who holds that ethical knowledge is synthetic a priori.)

Ayer has no patience for "absolutistic" ethical theories, which he characterizes as holding "that statements of value are not controlled by observation, as ordinary empirical propositions are, but only by a mysterious 'intellectual intuition'."[5] Ayer does not give any direct arguments against the existence of this faculty (but Moore did not give any very clear idea of what it is, or how it was supposed to work). Ayer's argumentative strategy here relies instead on the persuasiveness of his own alternate positive account of ethical language and cognition.

---

[4] Moore, Chapter 1.
[5] *LTL* 106.

Emotivism

Ayer writes:

> We begin by admitting that the fundamental ethical concepts are unanalysable, inasmuch as there is no criterion by which one can test the validity of the judgements in which they occur. So far we are in agreement with the absolutists. But, unlike the absolutists, we are able to give an explanation of this fact about ethical concepts. We say that the reason why they are unanalysable is that they are mere pseudo-concepts. The presence of an ethical symbol in a proposition adds nothing to its factual content. Thus if I say to someone, "You acted wrongly in stealing that money," I am not stating anything more than if I had simply said, "You stole that money."[6]

This conclusion is inevitable for Ayer given that he holds that there are no empirical verification procedures for ethical assertions.

But Ayer continues the paragraph quoted above with a positive account of what is happening when one produces ethical utterances:

> In adding that this action is wrong I am not making any further statement about it. I am simply evincing my moral disapproval of it. It is as if I had said, "You stole that money," in a peculiar tone of horror, or written it with the addition of some special exclamation marks. The tone, or the exclamation marks, adds nothing to the literal meaning of the sentence. It merely serves to show that the expression of it is attended by certain feelings in the speaker.[7]

It is important to recognize here that when he says that an utterance shows that the speaker has certain feelings, Ayer does not mean that the utterance *asserts* that the speaker has these feelings. Compare, for example, the autobiographical statement, "I feel moral disapproval of your action of stealing." This is the assertion that the speaker has certain feelings, and is true if and only if the speaker really does have those feelings. But when one says, "You acted wrongly in stealing that money," one *expresses* these feelings, but does not *assert that they exist*. The expression of these feelings is not an assertion at all, and is neither true nor false. Similarly, when one says, "I am enjoying eating these Brussels sprouts," this is true if one is sincerely reporting one's real state, but the expression of enjoyment, "Yum!!" is neither true nor

---

[6] *LTL* 107.
[7] *LTL* 107.

false. Ayer's view is that ethical utterances are like "Yum!!"—they express feelings, and do not report them. He calls this expressive function "emotive"[8] and his position on ethics is called "emotivism."

Ethical Disagreement

But one might object at this point that this account of ethical language does not get its function right. Ayer's claim is that the statement "That action is wrong" has the same function as "Ugh!!" and a different function from "The cat is on the mat." "Ugh!!" expresses negative emotion; "The cat is on the mat" makes an assertion which is either true or false. But this appears not to make sense of ethical disagreement. To see this, consider these two dialogues:

> **Dialogue 1:** **Fred** (while eating Brussels sprouts): Ugh!!
> **Sally** (while doing the same): Yum!!
>
> **Dialogue 2:** **Fred**: The cat is on the mat.
> **Sally**: No she isn't.

In **Dialogue 1**, Fred and Sally are expressing their contrary feelings about the Brussels sprouts, but there is no conflict, in the sense that they are not contradicting each other. A contradiction can occur between two sentences, logically speaking, only when the truth of one implies the falsity of the other. Nothing either true or false is being said by either, so there is no contradiction between these two utterances. They would not be tempted to discuss who is correct (or at least they should not). Correctness and incorrectness of utterances is a matter of their truth or falsity, respectively, and neither of these utterances is either true or false. In **Dialogue 2**, however, Sally is contradicting Fred. One or the other of them is correct. Now compare those two dialogues, in the respects indicated, with this one:

> **Dialogue 3:** **Fred**: That action is wrong.
> **Sally**: No it isn't.

The conflict indicated in **Dialogue 3** appears to be like the one in **Dialogue 2**, and unlike the one in **Dialogue 1**. In **Dialogue 3,** it appears that there is a genuine conflict, not just an expression of contrary feelings. Sally is *contradicting* Fred. A discussion of who was correct would be appropriate. But Ayer's emotivism claims that **Dialogue 3** contains utterances with functions identical to those in **Dialogue 1**. If emotivism fails to make sense of the undeniable fact that there is a conflict in **Dialogue 3** not present in **Dialogue 1**, it must be mistaken.

---

[8] *LTL* 108.

Ayer, however, adds some complications to his account of the function of ethical utterances, and these may answer this objection. He says:

> Ethical terms do not serve only to express feeling. They are calculated also to arouse feeling, and so to stimulate action. Indeed some of them are used in such a way as to give the sentences in which they occur the effect of commands. Thus the sentence "It is your duty to tell the truth" may be regarded both as the expression of a certain sort of ethical feeling about truthfulness and as the expression of the command "Tell the truth."[9]

Now, perhaps, we can explain the element of conflict in **Dialogue 3**: Fred and Sally have contrary feelings, and each is urging the other to feel differently. And because these feelings may issue in action, each is urging on the other contrary potential actions. But in contrast, in **Dialogue 1**, it seems, neither speaker cares very much whether the other shares his/her evaluation. Fred and Sally recognize each other's differences in taste, and neither wants the other to change. Neither is urging an action on the other that the other is disinclined to do.

Rational Ethical Argument

But here is a further objection not satisfied by this reply. One clear difference between the disagreements represented in **Dialogue 1** and **Dialogue 2** is that there is no rational process for adjudication of the difference represented in 1, whereas in 2, there typically is such a process available, at least in principle. When you and I disagree about the facts, we might be able to settle the matter rationally by taking another look, or by pointing out to each other things the other person might have missed, or by accumulating new evidence or discussing the weight of the evidence we accumulated, or by seeking the opinion of others. None of this is relevant in the case of the difference in 1. But ethical disagreement has the same possibilities for rational discussion and adjudication as clearly factual disagreement. Rational discussion and adjudication consists of the provision of good reasons to accept a genuine proposition *as true*. The reason no rational processes are available in the 1 is that there are only feelings involved, not beliefs about what is true—that there is no question about truth or falsity. So the fact that we can engage in rational discussion and adjudication over ethical differences such as the one in 3 shows that Ayer is mistaken, and that ethical

---

[9] *LTL* 108.

assertions really are cognitively meaningful, really do express propositions, really are capable of truth or falsity.

In reply to this sort of objection, Ayer attempts to give an account of rational ethical discussion consistent with his view:

> When someone disagrees with us about the moral value of a certain action or type of action, we do admittedly resort to argument in order to win him over to our way of thinking. But we do not attempt to show by our arguments that he has the "wrong" ethical feeling toward a situation whose nature he has correctly apprehended. What we attempt to show is that he is mistaken about the facts of the case.[10]

When we are arguing about whether an action is right, I could inform you about factual matters you might have been unaware of, such as the circumstances under which the action was done, or the agent's motives, or the consequences the action has already had, or the consequences one might expect it to have in the future, or the frequent consequences of that type of action. I hope that once you have recognized these additional facts, your evaluation of the action will change to match mine.

The important point here is that none of these facts has any relevance to your moral judgment unless you already have certain values concerning them. If you do not care, for example, about the fact that the action was done under duress, or that the action resulted in unhappiness for several others, then these facts will have no relevance to your evaluation of the action in question.

Ayer writes:

> In short, we find that argument is possible on moral questions only if some system of values is presupposed.... Given that a man has certain moral principles, we argue that he must, in order to be consistent, react morally to certain things in a certain way. What we do not and cannot argue about is the validity of these moral principles. We merely praise or condemn them in the light of our own feelings.[11]

The Consequences of Emotivism

Ayer perhaps exaggerates things somewhat when he describes what he takes to be the consequences of his position. He says:

---

[10] *LTL* 110-111.

[11] *LTL* 111-112.

> There cannot be such a thing as ethical science, if by ethical science one means the elaboration of a "true" system of morals. For we have seen that, as ethical judgements are mere expressions of feeling, there can be no way of determining the validity of any ethical system, and, indeed, no sense in asking whether any such system is true.[12]

But it appears consistent with Ayer's account of ethics that there is considerable scope for what might be called ethical science. If it happens to be the case that people share the same basic evaluative attitudes, then an ethical science could reveal the facts about which actions and arrangements would foster the satisfaction of these shared values. Practical ethics, conceived this way, would be a genuine empirical science, and would deal with questions that are by no means trivial or unimportant or easy to answer. Ayer himself unnecessarily dismissed this sort of intellectual activity as unworthy of philosophers, and for decades after the publication of *LTL*, academic philosophy departments, strongly influenced by Ayer's views, offered no courses on practical ethics. But the philosopher who was most closely associated with working out the details of Ayer's emotivism, C. L. Stevenson, once confessed to me in conversation that a long-standing desire of his was to teach a course in practical ethics, which he found valuable and intellectually challenging.

And there is a second sort of ethical science that is consistent with Ayer's emotivism. Suppose that the ethical feelings that people have are, on the whole, directed on particular occasions toward particular acts or states of affairs. One might wonder, then, whether there were any general patterns behind these particular reactions. Are there *kinds* of acts or states of affairs toward which I (or we) had similar evaluative reactions? A science of ethics could then take particular ethical reactions and attempt to discover their general laws. This is, of course, what any science does. Like the first job proposed for ethical science, this one is intellectually challenging, and would have, if successful, useful results.

But Ayer doubted that there were any such general patterns to be discovered, in his own case anyway:

> I suspect that my values do not significantly differ from the liberal values of John Stuart Mill, which means that they con-

---

[12] *LTL* 112.

tain a strong utilitarian element but they do not fit neatly, any more than his did, into a utilitarian mould.[13]

But even if all our (or one's) ethical reactions cannot be reduced to a simple set of general principles, thinking about principles is important to rational ethical thought. If someone accepts the general principle that actions of a certain sort are wrong, then there is reason to distrust our lack of negative reaction to particular actions that belong to that sort. On the one hand, particular reactions are the data justifying the adequacy of generalizations; but on the other, a well-established generalization can make us question a particular reaction not consistent with that generalization. So we adjust general principles and particular reactions to each other, aiming at an equilibrium containing more adequate general principles and particular responses. This is (roughly speaking) the picture of ethical theory presented to us by the influential contemporary moral philosopher John Rawls.[14] As I have presented it, it is completely consistent with thoroughgoing emotivism as Ayer presented it.

Evaluating Emotivism

What Ayer had to say about ethics attracted the most horror and dismay of anything in *LTL*—even more than his thoughts about religion. Ayer himself, it must be admitted, contributed to this by overstating his position somewhat. But a calmer look at what his theory entails and what it does not might have pacified his critics somewhat. Most notably, as we have seen, it does not dismiss ethical talk as pure nonsense, and Ayer certainly does not advocate that ethical writing be "committed to the flames." Nor does Ayer's theory rule out rational procedures for coming to, or debating, ethical positions; in fact, it offers, as we have seen, models for understanding what goes on in fully acceptable rational ethical debate.

What it does imply, however, is that it might be impossible rationally to settle some ethical disagreements—that agreement on all the facts might not suffice to remove some ethical divergence. This would occur when people had ground-floor differences in attitude about something; then ethical disagreement would survive all rational processes, which could serve only to settle factual disagreement.

---

[13] "Freedom and Morality," in *Freedom and Morality and other Essays* (Oxford: Clarendon Press, 1984) 49-50.

[14] *A Theory of Justice* (Cambridge: Harvard University Press, 1971).

But this is not as horrifying a prospect as it might at first appear. First, note that while emotivism allows this ground-floor disagreement as a possibility, it does not imply that it is reality. It is perfectly consistent with emotivism that everyone concerned with an ethical matter has sufficient similarity of basic pro- and contra- attitudes to make for ethical agreement, when all the facts were agreed upon. Recent work showing the evolutionary function of certain attitudes hints that similarity here might be biologically produced, innately, in all or most of us. And the fact that the circumstances of human upbringing do not differ hugely, on the whole, shows that it is possible that we have substantial similarity in learned values. Of course, there are some notorious ethical disagreements among people, but it might be that these could be resolved some day when more relevant facts are known, and more rational debate has taken place.

Second, even if it turns out, on the emotivist view, that no rational adjudication is possible for some ethical disagreements, this is not so bizarre a consequence as to rule emotivism out of consideration. No sensible theory of anything is so optimistic as to predict eventual rational solution of all disagreements in the area. Quinean considerations have the consequence that two contrary *scientific* theories might be equally well supported by all possible observations.

Imagine, then, a situation in which there are no empirical facts that serve to provide good reasons for one side of a moral disagreement and against the other. Emotivism denies that there is a *cognitive* disagreement here at all—denies, that is, that what one side says is true and the other false. But would it really make you more comfortable, in a case like this, to think that it is a matter of truth and falsity? Note that we assume that no empirical information is relevant to determination of which position is true and which false. Would you like to believe, as Moore does, that there is some strange non-empirical perception or "intuition" that is able to determine the real truth-values of these positions? How could you tell which of the disagreeing parties had intuited correctly? Would you trust intuition as a reliable way to determine truth? Would it be any different from just guessing, or relying on one's prejudice or non-rational feelings? Suppose then that you reject intuition as a method for determining the truth of ethical positions. What is left? Having ruled out empirical and non-empirical means, then (assuming that ethical statements are not analytic) we are left with statements without epistemologies—statements for which we have no way whatever to determine truth or falsity. What is the point of saying that

72

they are really true or false when there is no way, even in principle, for anyone to find out which?

The aspect of Ayer's ethics that seems so unbelievable to many philosophers is that on his view ethical utterances are neither true nor false; they never state facts. But perhaps the following considerations might make this more plausible. It appears that believing a fact is one thing, and being motivated to do an action is something else. Coming to believe a fact sometimes *produces* motivation, but it never *constitutes* motivation all by itself. So if holding an ethical view were merely believing something, it could not by itself be a motive for action. But if, instead, holding an ethical view is having an attitude, it *is* being motivated.

7

Skepticism and Knowledge

The Definition of 'Knowledge'

Ayer's ideas about what knowledge is and how one gets it are central to *LTL*, but only later does he deal with the philosophy of knowledge in detail: to some extent in his 1940 book *The Foundations of Empirical Knowledge*, but most comprehensively in *The Problem of Knowledge*, published in 1956.

In *PK*, Ayer begins with a definition of knowledge. '*S* knows that *p*' is true, he claims, if and only if:

1. *p* is true.
2. *S* is sure that *p*.
3. *S* has the right to be sure that *p*.

Condition 1 is uncontroversial; philosophers agree that if *p* is false, then nobody can be said to know that *p*. But what is interesting about this condition is that the fact that this condition obtains is not a feature of *S*'s subjective state, and cannot be determined by *S* through introspection. Compare **Condition 2**, which is a subjective state and can be accessed introspectively.

Condition 2 is a bit more questionable. To be sure that *p* is to believe *p* in a certain way, perhaps completely, with no residual doubt. But is belief of any kind a necessary condition for knowledge? Elsewhere,[1] Ayer considers the possibility of knowledge without belief in the cases of self-deception or temporarily forgetting something. In both cases, one might be said not to believe *p* at a time when one is not thinking about it, and perhaps cannot even retrieve it for the moment,

---

[1] "Knowledge, Belief and Evidence" in *Metaphysics and Common Sense* (London: Macmillan, 1969).

but at that time the knowledge that *p* is somehow still in one. Both cases do have philosophical interest; they tempt us to distinguish occurrent epistemological states—those actually going on in the conscious mind at a particular time—from latent ones—those stored and unconscious. Ayer, however, thinks that to call these cases "knowledge without belief" deviates considerably and unnecessarily from the ordinary usage of these terms, so he sticks with the requirement that knowledge requires belief.

But is it really a requirement that S be *sure* about *p*? Ayer's reason for saying this is again what he takes to be ordinary usage of the terms: he thinks that, when we are not completely certain of something, we say, "I believe it, but I don't *know* it." (One might question whether this really is ordinary usage.)

Condition 3 requires that *S* be justified in being sure that *p*. Ayer agrees with Hume that no empirical, contingent matter has for us more than some degree of probability, always short of 100%. It may be taken to follow that one is never justified in feeling complete certainty, in the sense of being immune from all possible doubt, about any contingent belief. If being sure is being completely certain in this sense, then **Condition 3** would entail that nobody would know any contingent truth. A skeptic might be willing to accept this odd conclusion, but Ayer is not. He insists that in any empirical matter there is always the possibility of going wrong, but he nevertheless thinks that we often have the right to be completely sure. To say that we have this right is not to say that we are infallible. It seems that what Ayer requires here is, rather, that one have enough justification for the rational person to consider the matter closed. To have genuine doubts, given this degree of justification, would not be rational; it would be neurotic. A neurotic, then, might really have sufficient justification for conclusive belief, fulfilling **Condition 3**, while still harboring doubts, thus failing **Condition 2**.

But it is still not completely clear that Ayer is right in his claims about the ordinary usage of 'knowledge' and 'belief.' Consider the cases in which there is less than conclusive justification for some proposition, but what justification there is makes that proposition quite likely. Imagine that some extremely reliable friend has promised to arrive at your house before 3 pm. You have very good evidence that she will do what she promised, but perhaps not conclusive evidence. You would count on her arrival, but you would not risk your life on it. Because of the small degree of doubt you have, you might not want to say that you *know* she will arrive before 3 pm. Would you say, then, "I *believe* that she will arrive before 3 pm, but I don't *know* it"? Or would this residual doubt mean that you give it considerable, but not conclusive credence—that you do not *fully* believe it? Well, perhaps we should not quibble here about small points of English usage. Nothing much hangs on this issue.

But there is a more significant problem with these conditions. Consider this example: There is an electric clock on my desk that has not lost a second since I have owned it, so I have a right to be sure that the time is what the clock says it is. This does not mean that what the clock tells me is infallible; it just means that the information it gives me is reliable enough so that I can consider the matter closed. On Monday morning I look at the clock, and the hands read 9:35, so I come to believe this is the time, and I am correct: it is 9:35. But unknown to me, the clock was unplugged exactly twenty-four hours before I looked at it, so it read the correct time by complete coincidence. It is 9:35; I am sure that it is 9:35; and I have a right to be sure, given the excellent reliability of that clock. All the conditions for knowledge are satisfied, but we would say I do not know that it is 9:35.

Examples like this last one were proposed by Edmund Gettier in a paper called "Is Justified True Belief Knowledge?"[2] These examples have come to be known as "Gettier examples" and have widely been accepted as showing that Ayer's definition, and others that define 'knowledge' as justified true belief, are inadequate. There is some controversy about how these definitions might be amended to take care of Gettier examples, and we need not go into details of this here, other than by pointing out that earlier, in *FEK*, Ayer gives this definition of 'knowledge':

> In the ordinary way, I think that all that is required for an empirical proposition to be known is that it should in fact be true, that no doubt should be felt about its truth, *and that the belief in it should not have been reached by way of a belief in any false proposition*, and should have good inductive grounds.[3]

My italics, added to this quote, indicate the part of this definition not in the later one we have been considering. It is curious that he left this part out of his later work; clearly when writing the *FEK* definition he had Gettier examples in mind,[4] and was trying to rule them out. In the ex-

---

[2] *Analysis* 1963.

[3] *FEK* 80.

[4] This was published 23 years before the Gettier article, so Ayer could not have called them this.

ample we considered above, the certain and justified belief in question, that it was 2:35, was "reached by way of" my false belief that the clock was working. This may be the way to deal with all Gettier-type counterexamples; but there is continuing controversy about the matter that we shall not go into.

There are several additional problems that arise surrounding Ayer's **Condition 3**. When does someone have the right to believe something? Presumably when the procedure that person used to arrive at the belief was a reliable one in general. As we have seen, Ayer's position does not demand that a procedure for arriving at a belief be infallible, so sometimes a reliable procedure will lead one to a false belief. What then makes a procedure a reliable one? It seems obvious that what should count as a reliable procedure is one that gives one true beliefs a large proportion of the time. But there is a problem here, which is illustrated by the following example. Suppose Fred has bought a lottery ticket, and his chances of winning are one out of a thousand. The draw is held, and he loses; afterwards, Sally says, "I knew you'd lose!" Could what Sally says be right? Of course, we can take her word that she felt sure that Fred would lose, and this belief turned out to be true, but was she justified in feeling sure? Did she even have sufficient justification to believe (never mind to be *sure*) that Fred would lose?

We might want to say here that she could not have had sufficient justification for being sure. The evidence she had—that there would be a fair draw from thousand tickets—is a highly reliable sign that a particular ticket will lose: it works 99.9% of the time. But if we want to say that she did not *know* that Fred would lose, perhaps this is not reliable enough.

Would even stronger evidence do? For example, if there were a million tickets? Perhaps no evidence is strong enough for knowledge. Maybe you would prefer to say that nobody can *know* that any particular ticket will lose in a lottery, although it may be extremely probable.

But consider, by contrast, this example: it seems natural to say that you know that when you turn the key in the ignition of your car, the car will start. But this is also a matter only of high probability; imagine that this happens only 999 times out of a thousand. Is there a difference here? What constitutes sufficient evidence to give knowledge is not at all clear.

Here is a second problem. Consider that clock on my desk again. It seemed that we should call the information it produced reliable, because electric clocks keep the time extremely well. But now, remembering the fact that the clock was unplugged, we might consider the information very unreliable, because electric clocks without a source of power tell the time extremely poorly. It seems that whether information counts as reliable depends on the classification we put things into, to judge the proportion of correct information. Classified as an electric clock, this thing is highly reliable. Classified as an unplugged electric clock, it is highly unreliable. Which one is the right classification? Why is that one correct? Until this question is answered, we do not know what to make of the notion of *reliable information*.

Skepticism

After discussing different sorts of skepticism in *PK*, Ayer concentrates on the kind of skeptical case that he finds the most philosophically interesting: in which the skeptical attack is directed against claims to knowledge based on inferences "in which we appear to end with statements of a different category from those with which we began."[5] Examples of skeptical arguments of this sort involve the claim that there is an illegitimate inference from sense experiences to claims about the existence of external physical objects, or of theoretical entities, or of other minds, or of the past. In all four cases, Ayer says, the skeptic argues in this pattern:

1. We depend entirely on inference from premises for the claims in question.
2. The inference in question is not deductive.
3. But the inference cannot be inductively acceptable either, for it carries us from what we experience to what we have no experience of at all.
4. Because these inferences are neither deductively nor inductively acceptable, they cannot be justified at all.

Step 3 here needs a bit of explanation. The inference that it will rain when we see dark clouds is fairly acceptable, because in our past experience rain often follows when there are dark clouds. But if we *never* experienced the association of these two things, then we would not be justified in this inference. But consider the case of our supposed knowledge of the external physical world. If all that is directly given to us is the contents of our own sensations, then we never experience the association between these sensations and external physical objects; so (the skeptic argues) the inductive inference from the existence of any sensations to the presence of any external physical objects is always unacceptable.

---

[5] *PK* 75-6.

The Sense-Data Theory

The reply to the skeptic that Ayer calls "naïve realist" denies **Step 1** above. The naïve realist claims that we have non-inferential perceptual knowledge: that in some sense we are, when perceiving, directly "given" the objects in question.

This is relevant only to the skeptical argument about our knowledge of the external world. We do not say that we now (literally) *see* an event that happened last year, or a thought in someone's mind, or an electron. But we do say that we see ordinary (present) physical objects, so naïve realism about our perception of these things seems obviously true. But Ayer argues at length that what we "directly perceive" is never a physical object, always rather subjective internal objects, called by various philosophers "ideas," "impressions," "presentations," "sensa," or, in Ayer's terminology, "sense-data."

Ayer first points out that in every case of visual experience, we seem to see something, whether there is that thing out there to be seen or not. For example, when you see an apple or hallucinate or dream one, you seem to see an apple. So, Ayer proposes, in every case there is a seeming-apple that you see; in other words, that the immediate object of your visual perception is a visual image, a sense-datum. He admits:

> What appears most dubious of all is the final step by which we are to pass from 'it seems to me that I perceive *x*' to 'I perceive a seeming-*x*' with the implication that there is a seeming-*x* which I perceive.[6]

Why not, then, just stick with ordinary ways of talking, in which one says "I seem to see an apple," rather than adopt Ayer's proposal for a strange way of talking, "I see a seeming-apple"? In his earlier *FEK*, he is explicit about why he advocates talking about things in this strange way:

> The philosopher who says that he is seeing a sense-datum in a case where most people would say that they were seeing a material thing is not contradicting the received opinion on any question of fact. He is not putting forward a new hypothesis which could be empirically verified or confuted. What he is doing is simply to recommend a new verbal usage.... If we accept this recommendation it will not be because our ordinary language is defective, in the sense that it does not furnish us with the means of describing all the facts, or in the sense that

---

[6] *PK* 105.

it obliges us to misdescribe some of them; but simply because it is not so good an instrument as the sense-datum language for our special purposes. For since in philosophizing about perception our main object is to analyse the relationship of our sense-experiences to the propositions we put forward concerning material things, it is useful for us to have a terminology that enables us to refer to the contents of our experiences independently of the material things that they are taken to present. [7]

This passage, published in 1947, shows that Ayer has come some distance from the verificationism central to *LTL*. The only sorts of justification recognized there were by word-meanings (for analytic sentences) and by sense experience (for synthetic sentences). But here, Ayer allows a third sort of justification. The reason that he urges that we accept sense-data talk is not that it is more highly confirmed by experience: he admits that sense-data talk and naïve-realistic talk are both empirically adequate—that is, that the superiority of sense-data theory is not a matter of being truer to the facts, as experienced. But neither is sense-data talk appropriate because of the conventions of ordinary usage; these, in fact, favor naïve realism. Ayer's criterion for truth here is something like usefulness in philosophical theory—a very different matter. In the next chapter, we shall talk more about this departure from Ayer's earlier commitment to a strict verificationism, and from his earlier views on the nature of philosophy.

Ayer's Oxford colleague J. L. Austin had launched an extended and effective attack on his sense-data theory, arguing that ordinary language was fully adequate for talking about perception, and that the need that Ayer thought he saw for creating sense-data was the result of his insensitivity to the varied and subtle uses and implications of ordinary talk. Austin's book on perception, *Sense and Sensibilia*, was not published until 1962, but Ayer found this ordinary-language objection stated in 1949 by Ryle:[8]

Ryle's comments on the everyday vocabulary of sensation and perception need not trouble [sense-data theorists]. It is not as if they were trying to give an account of the ways in which this vocabulary is commonly made to work. They need not even be suggesting that it is in any way inadequate for the ordinary

---

[7] *FEK* 25-6.

[8] Gilbert Ryle, *The Concept of Mind* (London: Hutchinson & Co., 1949)

purposes of communication. Their own talk of sense-data, assuming it to be legitimate, is obviously far less practical. What they are doing is to redescribe the facts in a way that is supposed to bring to light distinctions, of philosophical interest, which the ordinary methods of description tend to conceal.[9]

Ayer's hints at what reasons he thinks are good ones for accepting sense-data talk are not very detailed or persuasive. In *PK*, he says,

> We part company with [the naïve realist's position] by recognizing a distinction which he refuses to consider. For ... he denies, or overlooks, the existence of the gap between what things seem to be, in our special sense of seeming, and what they really are. His mistake, if it is one, is therefore just that he over-simplifies the situation; he denies the possibility of questions which can in fact be asked.[10]

But of course the naïve realist does make distinctions between how things seem and the how they are; this distinction is not made in terms of Ayer's "special sense of seeming," but why does it need to be? This is the question Ayer never seems to get around to answering.

The real disadvantages of sense-data theory, on the other hand, have been thoroughly aired in the literature. One of them is that sense-data are a strange kind of object. They necessarily appear only to one person; they never are other than they appear to be; they have no unnoticed features. Ayer admits that they are unlike ordinary objects, but does not regard these objections as decisive. He is right, of course, in claiming that these difficulties might be tolerated if they were indispensable features of the only adequate conceptual scheme for thinking about perception. But if Ayer fails to show us the necessity of theorizing his way about perception, then sense-data theory's odd ontology counts against it; even if it were not so odd, Ockham's razor councils us wisely to avoid unnecessary ontological excess.

But there is one problem that might be fatal to the theory, if Ayer cannot deal adequately with it. Suppose we accept Ayer's recommendation that we think about the objects of perception always as sense-data. It would seem that any knowledge of physical objects, then, must be inferred from what we perceive directly about sense-data. **Step 1** of the skeptic's argument is accepted. If the rest of the skeptic's argument goes through, then this conceptual scheme is in trouble.

---

[9] *PK* 108.
[10] *PK* 113.

Phenomenalism Again

But suppose that Ayer is right, and there is good reason for accepting **Step 1** of the skeptic's argument about perception. Does this mean that he must accept the argument's conclusion?

The phenomenalism Ayer accepted in *LTL*, if it could be made to work, would offer a good reply to the skeptic. Phenomenalism claims that every physical-object statement is equivalent in meaning to a set of observation-statements—statements about sense-data, according to Ayer's theory of perception. Because there is this meaning-equivalence, the inference from a set of statements about sense-data to physical-object statements is *deductive*—valid because of meaning equivalence, in the same way that the argument from the premise 'Fred is an oculist' to the conclusion 'Fred is an eye-doctor' is deductively valid. The phenomenalist defeats the skeptic's argument by denying **Step 2**.

But by the time he wrote *FEK*, Ayer had to admit that phenomenalism was flawed, because

> exact translations were not obtainable, owing to the fact that the sense-data in any given instance would belong to an indefinite and infinite range.[11]

Nevertheless, in *FEK* he still claimed

> in speaking of material things one was not doing anything other than express what would be mainly hypothetical propositions about sense data.[12]

By 1948, however, he had to admit that there were insuperable obstacles to giving even the outline of a translation of physical-object talk into sense-data talk.[13] Describing in *PK* what he takes to be the most general and telling argument against phenomenalism, he writes:

> If the phenomenalist is right, the existence of a physical object of a certain sort must be a sufficient condition for the occurrence, in the appropriate circumstances, of certain sense-data…. And conversely, the occurrence of the sense-data must be a sufficient condition for the existence of the physical ob-

---

[11] *MML* 89.
[12] *MML* 89.
[13] "Phenomenalism," *Proceedings of the Aristotelian Society*, 1947-8.

ject... The decisive objection to phenomenalism is that neither of these requirements can be satisfied.[14]

Considering the first claim, he argues, it is impossible to specify a set of conditions such that, given the truth of a physical-object statement, any observer must have a particular set of sense-data. So the presence of a yellow object does not entail the presence of a yellow experience, and it is impossible to present a complete list of the conditions which would make it entail this. A yellow object can produce an infinite variety of sense-data.

And regarding the second claim: the fact that no physical-object statement can be conclusively verified means that there is no finite set of sense-data statements that deductively entails any physical-object statement. For example, the fact that one has a yellow sense-datum does not entail that there is a yellow object out there; perhaps it is a white object under yellow light. But neither does the fact that one has a yellow sense-datum entail the hypothetical claim that if the light is white, there is a yellow object out there; perhaps one's eyes are abnormal (philosophers are fond of the example that if one has jaundice, white objects under white light result in yellow sense-data.) And it is useless to try to specify completely what should go in the "if" part of the hypothetical, that is, to spell out conditions so thoroughly that the presence of a yellow sense-datum does entail the presence of a yellow object, because there are an infinite number of different conditions that one would have to specify.

As we saw in Chapter 3, Ayer was aware of these objections to phenomenalism even at the time he was writing *LTL*; he was hopeful, however, that these objections could be overcome, and tried to do so in *LTL* and in the preface to the Second Edition of that book. But at some point Ayer, and most other philosophers attracted by phenomenalism, found the objections insuperable and gave up on the idea.

Phenomenalism would give Ayer a way of defeating the skeptic, by denying **Step 2** of his argument. Must Ayer then accept **Step 2**? And does that mean that his position must be prey to skepticism, as many critics of sense-data theory claim?

---

[14] *PK* 125.

Ayer's Answer to Skepticism

Ayer writes:

> The failure of phenomenalism does not mean, however, that
> there is no logical connection of any kind between the way
> physical objects appear to us and the way they really are.[15]

Even though the fact that there is something out there does not imply
that anyone will get any particular sense-data, it is, he claims, logically
impossible that there be no circumstances (actual or only hypothetical)
under which someone would experience that thing. And even though
the fact that one has X-ish experiences does not imply that there is an **X**
out there, or, indeed, anything at all out there, nevertheless it is, he
claims, "logically impossible for appearances to fool all the people all
the time."[16]

The first of these two claims is an attempt to save a weak form of
verificationism, despite the death of phenomenalism. It claims that
every real object (or at least every external physical object) is observable, and allows the disposal as nonsense of any claim about externals
that could not, even in principle, be related to observations. But this is
not to say that any particular observations are necessitated by the presence of an object. While observability might still be considered a test
for genuine meaningful assertions, at least for those putatively about
physical objects, having rejected phenomenalism Ayer can no longer
claim that verifying observations constitute the meaning of external-
object statements.

Ayer admits that there is no real set of observations that necessi-
tates the existence of an external object as observed. But his answer to
the skeptic comes from the second of his claims, that it is "logically
impossible" that the world never is as it is perceived.

Perhaps we can see this as an attack on **Step 3** of the skeptic's argument above. **Step 3** claims that we can have no reason to count
sense-data as evidence for the way the world is, but Ayer here appears
to be arguing that this is mistaken. The "logical truth" that we have to
be right sometimes means that sense-data do count as some evidence
about externals—though this evidence is always fallible.

A problem with both these "logical truths"—that every physical
object is observable, and that some inferences from sense-data to objects are correct—is that they do not appear to be logical truths at all.

---

[15] *PK* 130.
[16] *PK* 131.

Are they supposed to be made true merely by the definitions of the terms involved? Of which terms?

But even if we accept that these are logical truths, it does not seem that they provide a very substantial answer to skepticism. The main question Ayer faces is in dealing with the legitimacy of the inductive argument mentioned in **Step 3**. If Ayer is right about his "logical truths," then it is false that sense-data are *never* related to external objects, and a very weak conclusion may be drawn from their existence: that there is some sort of external world. But his "logical truths" do not establish the frequency of association between sense-data and external causes, so the strength of evidence for an external physical cause provided by any particular sense-datum is unknown, and might be vanishingly small: for all one knows, they might *almost never* be externally caused. Furthermore, these "logical truths" provide no reason at all to think that sense-data give any indication whatever of what the external world is like; so even if a red sense-datum gives reason to believe that something is out there, it gives no reason to think that it is red.

Has Ayer been successful in responding to the skeptic? Perhaps we should not expect too much progress here, on one of the oldest and least tractable philosophical problems, and Ayer never felt completely happy with his attempt in *PK*. Later, he described his procedure in that book this way: first he would allow the skeptic his premises, but then he would "take the verdict away from him, like a corrupt referee at a boxing match."[17] Quinton comments, "There is an air here of trying to settle an overdraft with a cheque drawn on the same account."[18]

---

[17] *MML* 123.
[18] Quinton 44.

8
The Job of Philosophy

Philosophy as Analysis

In *LTL*, Ayer devoted two chapters to explaining what he (then) thought the function of philosophy was. It was not, he argued, to provide substantive "first principles." An aspect of *LTL* that the old guard of philosophers found especially outrageous was Ayer's extended series of arguments that much of past philosophy was therefore illegitimate.

What does this leave for philosophers to do? They must, says Ayer, confine themselves to "works of clarification and analysis."[1] He goes on to explain that

> the philosopher, as an analyst, is not directly concerned with the physical properties of things. He is concerned only with the way in which we speak about them. In other words, the propositions of philosophy are not factual, but linguistic in character—that is, they do not describe the behavior of physical, or even mental, objects; they express definitions, or the formal consequences of definitions.[2]

This idea of philosophy as analysis was not new in Ayer; Russell and Moore had, earlier on, argued for much the same position. But Ayer's book made this idea enormously more widely known and believed. This picture of the proper job of philosophy took over English and American philosophy so thoroughly for a while that people began calling the typical philosophical style there "analytic philosophy," in contrast to the "speculative philosophy" done on the Continent.

---

[1] *LTL* 51.
[2] *LTL* 57.

How Can Analysis Inform?

Ayer's position is that philosophical truths are analytic, and thus without descriptive content, and, in a sense, vacuous. But it does not follow that they are trivial or obvious. They often are entirely unobvious, and take a great deal of skill and insight to unearth. How can this be the case? Presumably we all are competent users of the words the philosopher undertakes to analyze, so how can we fail already to know the analytic truths-by-definition that the philosopher sets out to discover and tell us?

Ayer attempts to answer this question by distinguishing two sorts of definition: an *explicit* definition, and a definition *in use*. The former defines a symbolic expression by giving another that is synonymous with it. This is what he supposes dictionaries do. But a definition *in use* of an expression

> shows how the sentences in which it significantly occurs can be translated into equivalent sentences, which contain neither the definiendum itself, nor any of its synonyms.[3]

We can count Ayer's attempt to define '*S* knows that *p*' discussed in Chapter 7 as an example of definition in use. It tells us how we apply a certain word or phrase—it gives us its application conditions. The odd thing is that one can know how to apply the phrase, that is, can distinguish perfectly well between occasions when it is appropriate to say 'I know that...,' 'She knows that...,' and so on, and occasions when it is not, but not be able to give an account of how this is done—of exactly what has to be true of people before they can be said to know something. An account of this sort, then, can be informative and even surprising.

A second answer to the question how the discoveries of philosophy can be analytic but unobvious is that philosophy provides not only definitions, but also the logical consequences of definitions and of sets of them. An analogy here is mathematics, which, Ayer supposes, consists entirely of analytic first principles (true by definition) and their logical consequences. Of course, even if the definitions are obvious to everyone, it does not follow that the consequences are similarly obvious. Advanced mathematics is the highly skilled activity of discovering the entirely unobvious logical consequences of these first principles.

Philosophy, then, for Ayer, can discover the unobvious, satisfying intellectual curiosity, but it can also have corrective power. We may

---

[3] *LTL* 60.

take something to be a consequence of the definition of a term when it is not; ambiguous terms may cause us confusion; we may misapply a term when we do not fully understand its application conditions. For example, it might be the case that people are widely mistaken in thinking that humans have free will, because they do not have a good idea of exactly what something must have for that term to apply to it. Once philosophical analysis has told us what the application criteria for the term 'free will' are, we might see that people lack what it takes to count as having free will—or that people have it. In either case, we would have made philosophical progress, and gained insight into what was previously unknown.

The Job of Philosophy: Second Thoughts

In *LTL*, Ayer reasoned that since philosophers are in no special position to undertake empirical investigation, a matter properly left to scientists, their discoveries must be analytic statements and their logical consequences—this is the only alternative. But later on, doubts arose.

The problem was this. The analytic truths he had supposed were the substance of philosophy owed their truth to the meanings of the words involved, and there was no other source for these meanings than the way the words were used by competent users of the language in everyday situations. But it became clearer to Ayer that ordinary usage was a messy matter, nowhere near adequate for the rigor and clarity desirable in a philosophical theory. So he gradually abandoned the view that philosophical truth is merely a consequence of ordinary linguistic usage, and started to see the philosopher's job as *reforming* ordinary language and conceptualization. Philosophers thus could be seen as stipulating new words, or new meanings for old ones, so as to provide clearer, less ambiguous, more adequate ways of speaking and conceptualizing.

This change in Ayer's philosophical methodology manifests itself even in his account of the status of the most basic principle in *LTL*, the verification criterion of meaningfulness. In its First Edition (1936), Ayer sanguinely assumed that this principle was an analytic truth—a consequence of the definition of 'meaning,' telling us the application conditions for that term, its definition in use. But in the Introduction to the Second Edition (1946), this is softened a little:

> In putting forward the principle of verification as a criterion of meaning, I do not overlook the fact that the word "meaning" is commonly used in a variety of senses, and I do not wish to deny that in some of these senses a statement may properly be

said to be meaningful even though it is neither analytic nor empirically verifiable. I should, however, claim that there was at least one proper use of the word "meaning" in which it would be incorrect to say that a statement was meaningful unless it satisfied the principle of verification.... Thus, while I wish the principle of verification itself to be regarded, not as an empirical hypothesis, but as a definition, it is not supposed to be entirely arbitrary.... I confess, however, that it now seems to me unlikely that any metaphysician would yield to a claim of this kind; and although I should still defend the use of the criterion of verifiability as a methodological principle, I realize that for the effective elimination of metaphysics it needs to be supported by detailed analyses of particular metaphysical arguments.[4]

Perhaps Ayer need not have yielded his ground here. The word 'meaningful' is used in various ways in ordinary language. Metaphysicians use it to apply to their pronouncements, but the fact that they say this does not mean that they are correct. They might be confused about the application conditions for the term; perhaps it is ambiguous, and their mistake might be corrected when philosophical analysis separates and clarifies the different meanings of the term. Ayer might then continue to rely on ordinary usage as the sole foundation for analyticity, and insist that the truths of philosophy are all analytic, without having to admit that metaphysically-inclined philosophers are correct when they count their pronouncements as meaningful in an appropriate sense. He may be giving up too easily.

Ayer does not explain what he means by recommending at the end of this quote that his general critique of metaphysics as "meaningless" be supplemented by "detailed analyses of particular metaphysical arguments." If the pronouncements in these arguments are, in some clear and relevant sense, meaningless, how can they be subject to detailed analysis?

In any case, a quote we have already examined from his 1956 work *The Problem of Knowledge* makes it clear that by then he no longer regards his job as philosopher to explain, disambiguate, or clarify ordinary usage at all. If one accepts his recommendation to use the way of speaking recommended by sense-data theory, he says,

> it will not be because our ordinary language is defective, in the sense that it does not furnish us with the means of describing

---

[4] *LTL* 15-16.

all the facts, or in the sense that it obliges us to misdescribe some of them; but simply because it is not so good an instrument as the sense-datum language for our special purposes.[5]

He acknowledges here that his claims about the existence of sense-data are not factual, subject to empirical verification, but neither are they analytic, based on the meanings given to terms in ordinary use. He takes it instead that what he is doing here is recommending a "new verbal usage," stipulating definitions for new terms, or recommending redefinition of old terms. What could be the motive for this? The ordinary use of ordinary terms, he tells us, is capable of describing all the facts, and forces no errors in describing them. The problem with ordinary usage is that it is not good enough "for our special purposes."

Ayer does not tell us much about what the special purposes of philosophy are, according to this later and considerably revised view. But perhaps he does not need to, because he has now come back to a much more familiar traditional philosophical position, which allows a considerable latitude in a priori pronouncement, diverging from ordinary language and conceptualization, to build a theory with philosophical adequacy.

Ayer's move away from his *LTL* view of the job of philosophy runs parallel with the decline of the popularity of the analytic method among English-speaking philosophers. Today, very few of them would identify their method as merely the provision of definitions of concepts and the consequences of these definitions. While Ayer was amending his own views, other philosophers were criticizing philosophical analysis from directions Ayer sometimes did not approve of. The most influential attacks came from "ordinary language" philosophy, centrally influenced by Wittgenstein and Austin, and from Quine.

Wittgenstein and Austin

As we saw earlier, Ayer and the Vienna Circle thought that their basic ideas—the verification criterion for meaning and the analytic method in philosophy—were traceable to Wittgenstein, who had been present at some meetings of the Vienna Circle, and whose early work, *Tractatus Logico-Philosophicus* (1922) was known to them. It was never easy to determine exactly what Wittgenstein really believed, but most interpreters now think that Ayer and the Vienna Circle took implications from the *Tractatus* that were quite far from its author's intentions; and that if Wittgenstein himself occasionally seemed to agree

---

[5] *FEK* 25-6.

with them, this was only a matter of his being very temporarily inclined to go along with their movement.

In later years, however, Wittgenstein's work and personal influence began very clearly to go in a different direction from Ayer's; and especially after the publication of *Philosophical Investigations* in 1953, Wittgenstein's thought was having widespread influence in producing quite a different philosophical methodology.

Philosophy-as-analysis presupposed that language was simply as a system of symbols with determinate meanings which mapped it on to the world, allowing us to refer to things and state facts. Wittgenstein and his followers emphasized, by contrast, the multitude of uses to which we put language and argued, in effect, that the narrow definitions-as-application-conditions that philosophical analysis aimed at discovering did not reveal anything like a significant picture of real-life language use.

As it became clear to Ayer that the Wittgensteinian philosophical program was quite different from his, Ayer continued to express respect for Wittgenstein's work, mixed however with frustration at figuring out exactly what his positions amounted to. And he continued to express fondness for the man personally, mixed however with a degree of exasperation at his neuroses.

> Though the manner of his disowning me... may have lessened my personal respect for Wittgenstein, it had not detracted from my admiration of him as a philosopher. I had looked forward eagerly to the appearance of his *Philosophical Investigations* and hoped that I should find in it at least some important clues to the solution of the philosophical problems on which I had been working. In this I was disappointed. This is not to say that I did not, and do not still, consider it a brilliant piece of work. When I dip into it, as I quite often do, I find almost every passage absorbing; when I try to recall what I have learned from it, I find that the gold dust which I thought that I was amassing has somehow slipped through my fingers.[6]

A significant figure in the growing Wittgensteinian movement was Ayer's Oxford colleague J. L. Austin, whose sensitive accounts of the multitude of functions of language made philosophers think that Ayer's *LTL* emphasis on fact-stating missed a great deal. His posthumous 1962 book *Sense and Sensibilia* is a sustained attack on sense-data theory, directed centrally against Ayer's *FET*.

---

[6] *MML* 93.

Neither Austin nor Wittgenstein presented substantial philosophical theories of their own. Both took the view that many of the standard philosophical problems arose when philosophers took an oversimplified view of language and conceptual structure, and that more careful and sensitive attention to these, and to (Wittgenstein emphasized) the whole way of life in which these were imbedded, would make these problems go away. In the view of Wittgensteinians, these problems called not for dissolution, not solution; not for theory but for therapy. In *MML*, Ayer quotes this excerpt from Wittgenstein:

> [Philosophical] problems are solved, not by giving new information, but by arranging what we have always known. Philosophy is a battle against the bewitchment of our intelligence by means of language.[7]

and comments:

> I think that my failure to profit from the later work of Wittgenstein goes together with my inability to acquiesce in this account of the scope and limits of philosophy.[8]

He reports that during the late 1930s, when he and Austin and some others met in a discussion group,

> Austin and I still shared much the same general outlook but very often differed on points of detail. His contributions to the discussions were mainly destructive.... I once said to Austin in exasperation, 'You are like a greyhound that refuses to race but bites the other greyhounds to prevent their racing either.' In later years he was to lead the pack, at measured speed, into the cul-de-sac of the study of ordinary usage, but his teeth never lost their sharpness.[9]

> Austin was a very clever man who had trained himself to capture the nuances of ordinary English usage. The best of his published papers...are fresh and imaginative. How much they contribute to the solution of the problems that trouble philosophers is disputable. I believe that Austin thought that they had made a substantial contribution, but also that this was not a matter that he greatly cared about, so long as his observations

---

[7] *Philosophical Investigations*, I, 109; quoted in *MML* 93-4.
[8] *MML* 94.
[9] *PML* 160-61.

about language were correct. His celebrated dictum 'Importance is not important; truth is' was sincerely meant.[10]

In a lecture delivered in 1961, Ayer sums up his later views about the Wittgenstein-Austin "ordinary language" movement this way:

> The insistence that ordinary language is perfectly in order has been a very useful corrective to the wilder flights of metaphysical speculation but, if taken too literally, it can lead to our letting things go by which might profitably be questioned and mobilizing in defense of what does not need defending.[11]

Ayer remarks that "Austin wanted to have disciples, and seemed to have succeeded" during the fifties; but "it is remarkable how evanescent his influence turned out to be."[12]

Quine

The "two dogmas of empiricism" criticized by Quine's hugely influential article with that name are the analytic/synthetic distinction and reductionism to sensation-language. As we have seen, these "dogmas" were at the center of philosophy-as-analysis, and Quine's article contributed greatly to its decline.

If Quine is right that there is no real analytic/synthetic distinction, then of course one cannot distinguish the job of philosophers from that of the rest of the cognitive community by saying that the former provide analytic truths, true by definition of the terms involved, whereas the latter provide empirical justification for purely synthetic truths. What, then, post-Quine, could the job of a philosopher be? Quine has not been terribly forthcoming about this, but we can speculate on what the answer to this question might be.

A distinction that does survive Quine's criticism is between a priori and a posteriori knowledge, though this becomes a relative matter of degree, rather than a strict bifurcation. The degree to which a proposition is a posteriori can be explained in terms of the degree to which it is susceptible of acceptance or rejection on the basis of experience. In his well-known metaphor:

> The totality of our so-called knowledge or beliefs...is a manmade fabric which impinges on experience only along the edges. ... A conflict with experience at the periphery occa-

---

[10] *MML* 187-88.
[11] *MML* 206.
[12] *MML* 188.

sions readjustments in the interior of the field. Truth values
have to be redistributed over some of our statements.... But
the total field is so underdetermined by its boundary conditions, experience, that there is much latitude of choice as to
what statements to reevaluate in the light of any single contrary experience.... Any statement can be held true come what
may, if we make drastic enough adjustments elsewhere in the
system. Even a statement very close to the periphery can be
held true in the face of recalcitrant experience by pleading
hallucination or by amending certain statements of the kind
called logical laws. Conversely, by the same token, no statement is immune to revision.[13]

The statements that are relatively likely to be chosen for revision given
recalcitrant experience, which Quine pictures at the "periphery" of this
field, are relatively a posteriori. Quine's example is "There are brick
houses on Elm Street."[14] Other statements, pictured as relatively centrally located, relatively immune from revision in the light of experience, relatively a priori, are the highly theoretical statements of physics
or logic or ontology. Quine does not mention philosophy here, but he
does incorporate in 'ontology' some traditional questions of philosophy, for example, the questions whether to count (for example) physical objects, forces, or classes as real. But he counts these questions as
"on a par with questions of natural science"—with the more highly
theoretical questions in natural science, that it. Both sorts of questions
are answered by the choice of a suitable cognitive scheme for dealing
with experience in some particular area. Both, therefore, have to take
experience into account. But both are largely underdetermined by experience. Additional "pragmatic" considerations lie behind the choice
among the innumerable conceptual frameworks logically available to
us, each consistent with all the experience we have in some area.

In this light, then, philosophy appears to be a high-level theory-
building enterprise, with other human activities as its subject matter.
Thus, for example, philosophers try to build theories of knowledge, of
ethical evaluation, of scientific practice, and so on. Philosophical
propositions are not, as the early Ayer thought, completely independent
of experience, and they do not rely exclusively on definitions rather
than also on facts. Quineans sometimes call philosophy seen in this
way "naturalized." This term indicates what they take to be philoso-

---

[13] Quine 42-3.
[14] Quine 43.

phy's continuity with natural science, and the relevance to philosophy of natural, empirical, matters-of-fact.

This view of philosophy, of course, is quite opposed to the view of philosophy as analysis Ayer defended in *LTL*; but, as we have seen, Ayer gradually retreated from a number of the central positions of that book during his long career following its publication. He appears gradually to have accepted at least some of Quine's criticisms. In 1973, Ayer concedes to Quine that "the propositions which constitute a theory do not confront the fact individually, but rather as a body."[15] In 1973 Ayer admits that admits that the boundary between analytic and synthetic truths is often "highly indeterminate"; but:

> Nevertheless, there are many cases in which it is generally agreed that two expressions are synonymous, or that one includes the other in its meaning, and so long as there is a considerable area in which it can be confidently applied, the distinction between propositions which are true on this semantic ground alone and propositions which confront the empirical facts does seem to be worth making.[16]

Similarly, he admits that the distinction between the definitions and the facts in a theory is "to some extent ... arbitrary," but:

> from the fact that the lines of demarcation may be drawn in various ways it does not follow that there is nothing which they demarcate.[17]

Ayer here does not yield entirely to Quine's views, but he is willing to go some way. So it would not be surprising if his methodology was influenced by Quinean considerations as well. When he says, for example, that philosophy of knowledge does not merely give definitions of the ordinary words we use in talking about knowing and perceiving, but rather provides a theoretical account of our activities, he may to some extent be influenced by a Quinean view of the assertions in a theory, neither reducible to experience-statements, nor definitional.

But Ayer was never again, after *LTL*, as explicit as he was in that book about what he came to take the methodology and purpose of philosophy to be. In 1984, he wrote, after rejecting Wittgenstein's account of what philosophy is for:

---

[15] *The Central Questions of Philosophy* (London: Weidenfeld & Nicolson, 1973) 201. Hereafter *CQP*.
[16] *CQP* 201.
[17] *CQP* 202.

> If asked what I should put in its place, I should be at a loss for
> any simple answer. the best I could achieve would be to put
> my own work in evidence.[18]

A Final Word

In 1936, when he published *LTL*, Ayer was in the vanguard of a revolutionary movement that was shortly to sweep through Anglo-American philosophy. His philosophical activity continued unabated until just before his death fifty-three years later, in 1989, but by that time, his work was far less central to the discipline's ongoing development. During the half-century he had retreated from the central positions of *LTL* in some substantial ways, and where he had not, the philosophical community had mostly moved without him. Nowadays, it is virtually impossible to find any philosophers who call themselves Logical Positivists.

But LTL is still a best-seller among philosophy books,[19] and the effects of Ayer's philosophical revolution are still obvious today. He moved Anglo-American philosophy permanently away from the windy idealist metaphysics that had dominated the field previously, and toward a more limited, rigorous, empiricist methodology.

His death was followed by a huge volume of laudatory assessment, in the mass media as well as in professional philosophical circles. But one is expected to say nice things about the departed, and the less-than-complementary comments are perhaps more revealing. Robert Jackson, Mrs. Thatcher's Minister for Higher Education, attacked him for "enormously narrowing the range of philosophical inquiry" and the philosopher Roger Scruton accused him of "destroying the conception in which the wisdom of humanity reposes."[20] The fact that he could attract such vituperative criticism more than fifty years after the publication of *LTL* shows how important and lasting Ayer's influence was. Assessments like these were, in a way, an appropriate memorial for Ayer, who always loved inciting intense controversy.

---

[18] *MML* 94.

[19] Amazon.Com, the on-line bookstore, reports that its recent sales have considerably outpaced anything by Wittgenstein, Austin, Quine or Kripke.

[20] Rogers 357.

Bibliography

During the 59 years of his philosophical career, Ayer published 23 books and just short of 300 articles. His books are listed below, with their original English publishers, but each has also been published in the U.S. The six books to which frequent reference is made are abbreviated in the text and footnotes by initials (*LTL, FEK, PK, CQP, PML, MML*), as indicated below.

For an exhaustive, well-annotated list of all his publications see "Bibliography of the Writings of A. J. Ayer," Compiled by Guida Crowley, Part Three of *The Philosophy of A. J. Ayer*, Lewis Edwin Hahn, ed. (La Salle, IL: Open Court, 1992).

Books

Language, Truth and Logic (London: Victor Gollancz, 1936. 2nd edition, Oxford: Oxford UP, 1946). Page numbers in this book refer to 2nd edition. [*LTL*]

The Foundations of Empirical Knowledge (London: Macmillan, 1940). [*FEK*]

Thinking and Meaning (his inaugural lecture as professor in the University of London) (London: H. K. Lewis & Co, 1947).

The Problem of Knowledge (London: Macmillan, 1956). [*PK*]

The Origins of Pragmatism (London: Macmillan, 1968).

Russell and Moore: The Analytical Heritage (London: Macmillan, 1971).

Probability and Evidence (London: Macmillan, 1972).

Russell (London: Fontana, 1972).

The Central Questions of Philosophy (London: Weidenfeld & Nicolson, 1973). [*CQP*]

Hume (Oxford: Oxford University Press, 1980).

Philosophy in the Twentieth Century (London: Weidenfeld & Nicolson, 1981).

Wittgenstein (London: Weidenfeld & Nicolson, 1985).

Voltaire (London: Weidenfeld & Nicolson, 1986).

Collections of Essays

Philosophical Essays (London: Macmillan, 1954).

The Concept of a Person and Other Essays (London: Macmillan, 1963).

Metaphysics and Common Sense (London: Macmillan, 1969).

Freedom and Morality and Other Essays (Oxford: Clarendon Press, 1984).

The Meaning of Life and Other Essays (Posthumous; London: Wiedenfeld & Nicolson, 1991).

Edited Anthologies

British Empirical Philosophers (with Raymond Winch. London: Routledge & Kegan Paul, 1952).

Logical Positivism (London: Geo. Allen & Unwin, 1959).

The Humanist Outlook (London: Pemberton with Barrie & Rockliff, 1968).

Memoirs

Part of My Life (London: Collins, 1977). [*PML*]

More of My Life (London: Collins, 1985). [*MML*]